THE **INS** AND **OUTS** OF
PREPOSITIONS

by
Jean Yates

BARRON'S

All inquiries should be addressed to:
Barron's Educational Series, Inc.
250 Wireless Boulevard
Hauppauge, New York 11788
http://www.barronseduc.com

Library of Congress Catalog Card No.: 99-21435

International Standard Book No. 0-7641-0757-7

Library of Congress Cataloging-in-Publication Data

Yates, Jean.
    The ins and outs of prepositions / by Jean Yates.
       p.   cm.
    Includes index.
    ISBN 0-7641-0757-7
    1. English language—Prepositions.   2. English language
Textbooks for foreign speakers.   I. Title.
PE1335.Y38   1999
428.2'4—dc21   99-21435
                                                 CIP

TABLE OF CONTENTS

* Two- or three-word combinations that function as prepositions

PART TWO: PREPOSITIONS BY FUNCTION

PART THREE: USING PREPOSITIONS

PART FOUR: ANSWERS AND GLOSSARY

INTRODUCTION

Prepositions pose more problems for the non-native speaker or learner of English than any other part of speech. Why? Prepositions are just little words that never change in form; they are pronounced softly, in unstressed syllables; they aren't even given capital letters in book titles; native speakers choose the correct ones without thinking. How can they be confusing?

The word "preposition" has a straightforward definition: a word placed before a noun or pronoun to define its relationship with another word in the sentence. For the learner of English, however, prepositions are anything but straightforward.

—Prepositions are difficult, if not impossible, to define without using other prepositions.
   Example:
   In the sentence, "The book is on the table," what does <u>on</u> mean?
   <u>On</u> means "*above* and supported *by*."

—In no other language are the prepositions (if they exist at all) the exact equivalents of English prepositions.
   Example:

Spanish	*English*
Vive <u>en</u> Washington.	He lives <u>in</u> Washington.
Vive <u>en</u> la Avenida New Jersey.	He lives <u>on</u> New Jersey Avenue.
El está <u>en</u> el aeropuerto.	He is <u>at</u> the airport.
Estoy pensando <u>en</u> ti.	I am thinking <u>about</u> you, or
	I am thinking <u>of</u> you.

—Many preposition words can also be adverbs or conjunctions.
   Examples:

the preposition <u>down</u>	She walked <u>down</u> the hill.
the adverb <u>down</u>	He put the book <u>down</u>.
the preposition <u>after</u>	She took a nap <u>after</u> lunch.
the conjunction <u>after</u>	She went outside <u>after</u> she put the book down.

—Many prepositions can indicate more than one meaning or relationship.
   Examples with <u>after</u>:

later than	We rested after lunch.
in pursuit of	The cat is after the mouse.
because of	He was angry after the way she acted.
in the style of	This is a painting after Picasso.
continuously	She worked night after night.

—Two or more prepositions can have the same meaning.
    Sometimes these prepositions are interchangeable.
    Examples:
        She is disappointed <u>in</u> her new job.
        She is disappointed <u>with</u> her new job.
    Sometimes they are not interchangeable.
    Examples:
        He is fascinated <u>with</u> his new job. (but not *in*)
        He is interested <u>in</u> his new job. (but not *with*)
        He is bored <u>by</u> his new job. (*by* or *with*, but not *in*)

—Many prepositions are also used in expressions where their meaning is entirely different from any of their predictable meanings. Expressions like this do not follow any pattern or logic, and do not allow for substitutions. They must be learned as vocabulary units.
    Examples: It's <u>about time</u>.
                They are never <u>on time</u>.
                She got here <u>in time</u> to see the whole show.

—A preposition in combination with another word may have multiple meanings.
    Example:

<u>make up</u> your bed	-arrange
<u>make up</u> your face	-paint
<u>make up</u> your mind	-decide
<u>make up</u> a story	-invent
<u>make up</u> a list	-write down
<u>make up</u> the difference	-equalize
<u>make up</u> last week's homework	-do overdue work
<u>make up</u> for lost time	-compensate
<u>make up</u> with your girlfriend	-reestablish a relationship

—Different prepositions can follow the same verb to change its meaning completely.
    Example:

break <u>down</u>	-collapse
break <u>in</u>	-enter by force
break <u>off</u>	-remove
break <u>out</u>	-erupt
break <u>out of</u>	-leave by force
break <u>through</u>	-establish a successful idea
break <u>up</u>	-end a relationship

—New preposition combinations continue to become part of the language.
    Examples:

<u>boot up</u>	-restart a computer

| key in | -type text on the computer |
| log on | -connect to the Internet |

—Preposition words are sometimes "made into" other parts of speech.
  Examples:

prepositions as nouns	I want to learn the ins and outs of prepositions.
prepositions as adjectives	The hospital has only a few in patients. There is a down side to his idea.
prepositions as verbs	I heard they were upping the price.

As if all this weren't enough, English sentence patterns can also be troublesome, especially when prepositions are involved. The use of articles and pronouns and the formation of questions, adjective clauses, and noun clauses can be tricky.

The Ins and Outs of Prepositions is designed to take the mystery out of prepositions for those whose first language is not English. It is a comprehensive handbook and guide that explains in detail the 61 commonly used English prepositions and their usage. It is easy to read and understand, and easy to use for quick reference or for more serious study.

Part One consists of a chapter for each of the prepositions. Each chapter includes all of the predictable definitions of the preposition, with typical grammar patterns, example sentences, and lists of the verbs and nouns that are most often used for each meaning. Idiomatic expressions and phrasal verbs are also defined and illustrated with examples.

Part Two provides charts and diagrams that illustrate and compare the functional usage of different prepositions. Each section includes exercises and answers that will help the reader remember the guidelines.

Part Three gives formulas and examples that describe the use of prepositions before pronouns and verbs, in adjective and noun clauses, in questions, in separable and nonseparable combinations with verbs, and as other parts of speech. Exercises at the end of each chapter provide practice with these patterns.

Part Four is an alphabetical list of over 3800 common adjectives, nouns, and verbs with the prepositions that normally precede and/or follow them, with the preposition name and section number of the text where the expression can be found, for further explanation of its meaning and use in a sentence.

Use this book to help yourself become more familiar with the patterns of English sentences. Train your ear to hear prepositions in conversations, and your eye to see them when you read. Ask yourself if you know the underlying meaning of each one. By all means, add new words you hear to the lists in the sections where they belong, and write down new expressions and phrasal verbs as you come across them. Mastering English prepositions is a challenge, but a valuable skill that will enhance your understanding and help you express yourself with confidence.

PART ONE: THE PREPOSITIONS

HOW TO USE PART ONE

Each definition of a preposition is followed by one or more *patterns*, which indicate the word order appropriate for the definition.

The verbs in each pattern can be changed to other tenses.

Example:

Pattern: verb + toward + noun
The money goes toward helping the family.

This could also be:
The money went toward helping the family.
The money will go toward helping the family.
The money is going to go toward helping the family.

When a word cannot be substituted, that word is included in the pattern.

Example:

Pattern: *be* + after + noun
The reception is after the wedding.
be is the only possible verb for this pattern.

When a word is optional, it is in parentheses.

Example:

Pattern: *be* + outside (of) + noun
The dog is outside the house.
The dog is outside of the house.

When the word *noun* is in the pattern, use the normal patterns for noun usage, as outlined in Part Three.

Example:

Pattern: verb + against + noun
Dr. Jones is against the idea.

This could also be:
Dr. Jones is against my idea.
Dr. Jones is against this idea.
Dr. Jones is against our ideas.
Dr. Jones is against some of their ideas.

When the noun determiner cannot be substituted, it is included in the pattern.

Example:

Pattern: verb + against + the + noun
We sailed against the wind for an hour.
(*the* cannot be replaced by *a, this, my,* or any other word)

When the word *one's* is in the pattern, it can be replaced by any possessive adjective (*my, your, his, her, its, our, their*)

Example:

Pattern: to + one's + noun
Someone will come to your aid.
Someone will come to his aid.
Someone will come to our aid.

When no noun determiner is used, the symbol ø is in the pattern.

Example:

Pattern: verb + against + ø + noun
I drive against traffic every morning.

The typical verbs, nouns, and adjectives listed with each pattern are the most common words that are used with the preposition. It is a good idea to think of the combinations as units. As an exercise, you may wish to write sentences with the suggested words, following the pattern and keeping the meaning of the combination in mind.

❶ About identifies a **topic.**

Pattern 1: noun + *be* + about + noun
This book is about prepositions.
Nouns commonly used before about:
  argument, article, book, conversation, disagreement, discussion, joke, lecture, movie, news, play, program, report, speech, story

Pattern 2: noun + about + noun
She gave me advice about my loan.
Nouns commonly used before about:
  assurance, complaint, comment, gossip, lie, question, statement, truth

Pattern 3: **verb + about + noun**
He often talks about his job.
Verbs commonly used before about:
  agree, argue, brag, care, complain, cry, do, dream, forget, groan, hear, joke, know, laugh, lie, moan, pray, read, say, scream, sing, talk, think, wonder, worry, yell

Expressions:
  to see about—
  1. to delay a decision until more information is known
     We want to buy a house, but we will see about that later.
  2. to get information about
     I called that office to see about getting a job there.
  to find out about—to get information about
     She called the school to find out about her daughter's behavior.

Pattern 4: verb + noun + about
She knows something about airplanes.
Typical verbs used with this pattern:
  ask, find out, know, learn, say

Typical nouns used before about:
  a little, a lot, quite a bit, nothing, something, very little

Pattern 5: verb + indirect object + about + noun
They asked me about my trip.
Verbs commonly used with this pattern:
  advise, ask, bother, contact, harass, question, remind, teach, tell, write

Pattern 6: adjective + about + noun
They were very kind about our late arrival.
Adjectives commonly used before about:
  charming, kind, nasty, nice, mean, rude, sweet, understanding, unkind

❷ About can identify the **cause of an emotion or condition.**

Pattern: adjective + about + noun
We are excited about our vacation.

Adjectives commonly used before <u>about</u>:
    angry, anxious, bashful, concerned, confused, crazy, excited, glad, happy, mad, nervous, objective, optimistic, pessimistic, right, sick, silly, unhappy, upset, worried

❸ About (adverb) can mean **approximately.**

Pattern: about + number
It is about nine o'clock.
We have about ten dollars each.

❹ About can mean **in all parts of.**

Pattern 1: *be* + noun + about + noun
There is a lot of excitement about town.

Pattern 2: past participle of verb + about + noun
Papers were scattered about the house.
Typical past participles used before <u>about</u>:
    scattered, sprinkled, strewn, thrown

❺ About can **describe a noun.**

Pattern: *something/nothing* + (adjective) + about + noun
There is something about her that I like.
There is something adorable about her.
There is nothing nice about that.
Adjectives commonly used before <u>about</u>:
    adorable, attractive, bad, cute, exotic, fascinating, familiar, fishy, funny, good, interesting, nice, peculiar, special, strange, unusual, weird, wonderful

❻ About can mean **in all directions.**

Pattern 1: motion verb + about + noun
We wandered about town for a few hours.

Pattern 2: motion verb + about (adverb)
The baby crawls about the house.
Verbs commonly used with these patterns:
    crawl, go, jump, look, move, poke, run, walk, wander

❼ About (adverb) can mean **almost.**

Pattern: *be* + about + adjective
She is about ready.
Adjectives commonly used after <u>about</u>:
    complete, done, finished, perfect, ready, right, through

❽ Expressions

about + infinitive—ready to
The show is about to begin.

to be about time—an expression of annoyance that a person or thing has arrived late.
"It's about time you got here," said the mother when her daughter came home late.

to have an air about one—to seem uncaring or unfriendly
That new guy has an air about him.

not about (adverb) + infinitive—not willing to
I'm not about to sign that agreement.
They're not about to go home early.

about face
    1. (verb) a military command to turn halfway around, and face the opposite direction
       The sergeant ordered, "About face!"
       He told his men to about face.
    2. (noun) a complete change of opinion
       He did an about face when he learned the facts.

❾ Phrasal verbs

bring about (separable)—cause
The storm brought about problems.
The storm brought them about.

come about (intransitive)—happen
How did that situation come about?

to get about (intransitive)—to be able to walk
He is ninety years old, and he gets about very well.

to find out about (nonseparable)—to get information or news about something
When did you find out about the accident?

2 · ABOVE

❶ Above can mean **in or at a higher place.**

Pattern 1: *be* + **above** + **noun**
A dark cloud was above the house.

Pattern 2: **verb** + **noun** + **above** + **noun**
Let's hang the picture above the sofa.
Verbs commonly used before above:
arrange, carry, hang, hold, keep, place, put, set

❷ Above can mean **at a higher level, value, or rank.**
Her blood pressure is above normal.
The children in her class are all above average.
In the navy, a captain is above a commander.

❸ Above (adverb) can indicate something **written earlier** in a book, article, or other document.
Please see the instructions above.

❹ Above (adjective) describes something written earlier.
Please follow the above instructions.

❺ Above indicates that a person is **too good** to commit the stated negative action.

Pattern 1: *be* + **above** + **noun**
The policeman is above cruelty.
Nouns often used after above:
cruelty, dishonesty, meanness, perjury, theft, murder, treason

Pattern 2: *be* + **above** + **verb in gerund form**
He may be poor, but he is above stealing.
Gerunds often used with this meaning:
breaking the law, cheating, gossiping, lying, robbing, snooping, stealing

❻ Expressions
up above (adverb)—in heaven
Our dear grandmother is now in peace up above.

above and beyond the call of duty—action that is more or greater than what is expected of a person
My teacher's help after school was above and beyond the call of duty.

above board—completely honest and open
Our negotiations with the company were above board.

above the law—exempt from restrictions of the law
People in power sometimes believe they are above the law.

① **Across** indicates the direction of **movement from one side of an area to the other.**

Pattern: motion verb + across + noun
The girl ran across the yard.
Verbs often used before <u>across</u>:
crawl, drive, go, limp, move, ride, run, swim, walk

② **Across** can mean **on the other side of** a place.

Pattern: verb + across + noun
My friend lives across the street.

③ **Across from** means **opposite** or **facing.**

Pattern 1: verb + across from + noun
My assistant's office is across from mine.
My secretary sits across from me.

Pattern 2: verb + across + noun + from + noun
My assistant's office is across the hall from mine.

④ **Across** and **all across** mean **in every area of.**
People across the world are using the Internet.
There is a heat wave all across the country.

Expression:
across the board—including everyone or everything
Everyone got a raise in salary: there was a wage increase of three percent across the board.

⑤ **Phrasal verbs**
come across (nonseparable)—find something unexpectedly
I came across this old picture of you when I was looking for some documents.
come across (intransitive)—be received by an audience
The banquet speaker was not sure how well he came across.
run across (nonseparable)—to find something unexpectedly
I ran across a letter you wrote to me when we were children.
get (something) across to (separable)—make something understood
The young girl tried to get it across to her boyfriend that she was not ready to get married.

4 · AFTER

❶ After means **later than** or **following.**

Pattern 1: *be* + after + noun
The reception is after the wedding ceremony.

Pattern 2: after + gerund form of verb + noun
After finishing your homework, you can watch television.

Pattern 3: after (conjunction) + subject noun + verb
After you finish your homework, you can watch television.

Pattern 4: verb + after (conjunction) + subject noun + verb
The boss left after I came in.

❷ After can mean **lower in value or rank.**

That school's athletes placed after ours in the playoffs.

❸ After can mean **in pursuit of.**

Pattern: verb + after + noun
The cat ran after the mouse.
Verbs often used before <u>after</u>:
be, come, go, run

❹ After can mean **because of.**

Pattern: adjective . . . + after + noun
He was mad at her after her behavior at the party.
Typical nouns used after <u>after</u>:
attitude, behavior, failure, kindness, manners, outburst, reaction, success

❺ After can mean **in spite of.**

Pattern: after + verb in gerund form
They never got married, after dating for years.
After reading this article three times, I still don't understand it.

❻ After can mean **in the style of.**

Pattern: noun + after + noun
The school play was a drama after Shakespeare.

❼ After can indicate **continuously.**

Pattern: time period + after + same time period
The man waited night after night for his telephone to ring.
Life got harder year after year.
His mother told him time after time to clean up his room.
Nouns often used with this meaning:
day, hour, month, night, time, week, year

❽ Expressions

after all
  1. in spite of what happened; nevertheless
     Our best player got hurt in the first quarter, but we played hard and won the game after all.
  2. as a justification
     Of course I am tired; after all, I have been working for twelve hours.

after all is said and done—eventually
  I know you feel bad now, but you will be glad about this after all is said and done.

after one's own heart—especially appreciated
  Her mother always serves us chocolate cake; she is a woman after my own heart.

❾ Phrasal verbs

look after (nonseparable)—take care of something or somebody
  She looks after our baby on weekends.

take after (nonseparable)—be similar to an older relative
  The baby takes after his father.

to name after (separable)—give a baby the name of someone special
  They named the baby after his grandfather.

5 · AGAINST

❶ Against means **touching** something or somebody for support.

Pattern 1: verb + against + noun
The man was leaning against his car.
Typical verbs used before against:
hang, lean, lie, rest, sleep

Pattern 2: verb + noun + against + noun
They held the mirror against the wall.
Typical verbs used before against:
butt, hold, keep, lay, lean, place, pull, put, rest, set

❷ Against means **touching forcibly.**

Pattern: noun + verb + against + noun
The rain beat against the window.
Verbs often used before against:
bang, beat, crash, crush, heave, hit, knock, push, splash, throw, thrust

❸ Against means **in opposition to.**

Pattern: noun + verb + against + noun
The mayor was against the idea of a new day-care center.
Stealing is against the law.
Our senator voted against that bill.
Typical verbs used before against:
act, argue, campaign, debate, fight, go, move, play, vote, work
Nouns often used after against:
action, bill, concept, enemy, force, idea, law, nomination, orders, plan, precepts, principles, proposal, regulations, religion, rules, suggestion, teachings, team, wishes

❹ Against can mean **toward a force in the opposite direction.**

Pattern: verb + against + the + noun
Sailing was rough yesterday; we sailed against the wind all day.
Typical verbs used before against:
drive, fight, go, move, run, sail, struggle, swim, walk
Nouns often used after against:
current, flow, force, tide, wind

Expression:
against traffic—
I drive against traffic because I live in the city and I work in the suburbs.

❺ Against can mean **to the disadvantage of.**

Pattern: noun + *be* + against + noun
You may not get that job because your age is against you.

Typical nouns before <u>be against</u>:
age, background, height, inexperience, nationality, youth

⑥ Against can mean **in contrast to.**
It is hard to see your black necklace against that dark dress.

⑦ Against can mean **in defense of.**

Pattern: verb + noun + against + noun
They vaccinated the children against whooping cough.
Their heavy coats protect them against the cold.
Typical verbs before <u>against</u>:
guard, lock up, protect, seal, vaccinate

⑧ Against can mean **in partial payment of.**

Pattern: noun + against + noun
Enclosed is a check for $100 against my bill.
Typical nouns after <u>against</u>:
balance, bill, charges, debt, loan

⑨ Expressions

against all odds/with all odds against one—having very little chance of success
Team A was less experienced than Team B, but they won the game against all odds.
Many people come to this country and become successful with all odds against them.

go against the grain—seem very wrong
Child abuse really goes against the grain.

have two strikes against one—be at a strong disadvantage (In baseball, a player is eliminated after three strikes.)
When you are poor and sick, you have two strikes against you.

⑩ Phrasal verb

be up against (nonseparable)—be faced with opposition, trouble, or hard work
My friend is up against a lot of problems.
When he started his own business, he had no idea what he was up against.

6 · AHEAD OF

❶ Ahead of means **closer to a destination than** or **in front of.**

My friend arrived first, and was ahead of me in line.

❷ Ahead of means **before.**

You are in a hurry; please go ahead of me.

❸ Ahead of can mean **more advanced than.**

Because he was absent for two weeks, the other students in his class are ahead of him.

❹ Phrasal verbs

get ahead (intransitive)—succeed
She has struggled all her life to get ahead.

get ahead of (nonseparable)—advance faster or further than someone else
They are rivals, always competing to get ahead of each other.

go ahead (intransitive)—Do it; begin now
I asked for permission, and they told me to go ahead.

❶ Along means **following the boundary** of something.

Pattern: verb + along + noun
We walked along the water's edge at the beach last night.
Typical verbs before along:
jog, stroll, run, walk

❷ Along with means **together.**

Pattern: verb + along with + noun
He used to sing along with me.
Typical verbs used before along with:
hum, play, run, sing, walk, work

❸ Expressions

all along (adverb)—the whole past time
They have been enemies all along.

❹ Phrasal verbs

get along (intransitive)—live together in harmony
She and her old roommate didn't get along.

get along with (nonseparable)—to live in harmony with someone
I hope she gets along with her new roommate.

8 · AMONG

❶ Among can mean **surrounded by.**

Pattern: verb + among + plural (three or more) noun
They camped in the woods among the trees.

❷ Among can mean **with each other.**

Pattern: verb + among + plural (three or more) noun
The children quarreled among themselves.
Typical verbs before <u>among</u>:
argue, celebrate, debate, discuss something, fight, play, share something, talk

❸ Among can mean **to the individuals in a group.**

Pattern: verb + among + plural (three or more) noun
They distributed the flyers among the students.
Typical verbs before <u>among</u>:
distribute, hand out, pass out

❹ Among can mean **included in a group.**
Your friends are among the survivors.

❺ Among can indicate **many of a group.**
Latin dancing is popular among the college students.

❶ Around means **following a boundary, in a circular direction.**

Pattern: motion verb + around + noun
We walked around the block.
Verbs commonly used before <u>around</u>:
drive, fly, race, ride, run, skip, travel, walk
Nouns commonly used after <u>around</u>:
block, building, house, room, track, world

❷ Around (adverb) indicates **movement in a circular direction in place.**

Pattern: verb + around (on)
The earth spins around on its axis as it travels around the sun.
Typical verbs used before <u>around</u>:
spin, turn, whirl

Expressions:
  1. **turn around** (adverb)—face the opposite direction
       You are going east; to go west, you have to turn around.
  2. **turn something around** (adverb)—reverse the position of something
       Turn your chair around and talk to me.

❸ Around means **enclosing.**

Pattern: verb + noun + around + noun
The teacher drew a circle around each mistake.
The rancher put a rope around the cow's neck.
Verbs commonly used with this pattern:
draw, fasten, put, tie, wrap

❹ (All) around means **in all areas of.**
There is crime all around this city.

❺ (All) around can mean **on all sides of.**
People were screaming all around me.

❻ Around means **on another side of.**
The bank is around the corner.
Their farm is just around the bend.
Expressions:
  1. **around back**—at the back of a building
       Go around back to pick up your merchandise.
  2. **go around the bend**—be crazy
       I am so busy, I think I am going around the bend.

❼ Around (adverb) means **approximately.**

Pattern: around + number
We have around twenty dollars in our pockets.
I'll see you at around three o'clock.

❽ (All) around can mean **in many directions, randomly**

Pattern: motion verb + around + noun
The new teacher looked around the room.
Verbs often used before around:
   drive, flit, go, jump, look, march, move, play, run, search, shop, snoop, walk, wander

❾ Around can mean **do nothing.**

Pattern: verb + around + place
Those teenagers just hang around the mall with nothing to do.
Verbs used before around:
   drag, fool, goof, hang, lie, lurk, mope, sit

❿ Expression

give someone the runaround—avoid taking action by giving long explanations
   When I tried to return my broken air conditioner, the store manager gave me the runaround.

⓫ Phrasal verbs

get around (intransitive)—often visit a lot of places and meet a lot of people
   He seems to know everybody; he really gets around.

get around to (non-separable)—finally make the effort to do something
   One day I will get around to cleaning out my files.

kick somebody around (separable)—mistreat someone by controlling him or her
   He left that job because the boss always kicked him around.

kick something around (separable)—consider the pros and cons of an idea
   We are kicking around the idea of moving to Florida.

show someone around (separable)—take someone on a tour of a place
   He showed me around the campus when I first arrived.

hang around with someone (nonseparable)—often be with someone
   She hangs around with a boy who lives up the street.

run around with someone (nonseparable)—often go out with someone
   She is running around with a new group of friends.

❶ As means **in the role of.**

Pattern 1: verb + as + noun

She is a trained teacher, but she works as a secretary in our office.

Typical verbs used before as:

act, serve, substitute, volunteer, work

Pattern 2: verb + noun + as + noun

We have selected you as the captain of the team.

Typical verbs:

choose, elect, nominate, pick, select, use

❷ Expression

as for me—regarding me

They all went to the movies; as for me, I stayed home.

11 · AT

① At can indicate **location**

Pattern 1: at + the + place within a city or town
The women are at the supermarket.
Nouns commonly used with this pattern:
   apartment, bus stop, factory, hospital, hotel, house, mall, office, park, parking lot, restaurant, station, store, theater, university

Pattern 2: at + an address
She lives at 3757 North 52nd Street, apartment 10.
You can contact him by e-mail, @xyz.com
(The symbol @ is pronounced "at.")

Pattern 3: at + the + place within another place
He was waiting in the room at the door.
He likes to sit in her apartment at the window facing the park.
Nouns commonly used with this pattern:
   counter, desk, table, window

② At indicates a **place of attendance.**

Pattern 1: *be* + at + ø place or meal of regular attendance
The children are at school.
We aren't allowed to watch television when we are at dinner.
Nouns used with this pattern:
   church, class, home, practice, school, work
   breakfast, lunch, dinner

Pattern 2: *be* + at + noun of event
They are at the movies.
She is at a meeting.
Nouns commonly used with this pattern:
   breakfast, brunch, celebration, concert, conference, dance, debate, dinner, forum, function, funeral, game, lecture, luncheon, meeting, movies, parade, party, play, program, reading, reunion, show, wedding

③ At can indicate **in the direction of; toward.**

Pattern 1: verb + at + noun
The teacher smiled at the new girl.
Verbs commonly used with this pattern:
   aim, frown, glare, grab, grin, growl, hit, howl, laugh, leer, look, rush, shoot, shout, slap, smile, snatch, stare, swear, swing, wink, yell

Pattern 2: verb + noun + at + noun
The small boy threw a rock at the window.
Typical verbs:
   swing, throw, toss

Expression with this meaning:
make a pass at—indicate romantic interest toward
The young man made a pass at the beautiful woman he met at the party.

❹ At is used to express **time.**

Pattern: at + specific time
We are leaving at four thirty.
They went home at midnight.
We always eat lunch at noon.

Expressions with this meaning:

at first—when something started
At first we thought this hike would be easy.

at night—when it is night
I always read or study at night.

at once—immediately (see also *number at a time,* below)
We must pack up and leave at once.

at present—now
At present they are sleeping.

at last—finally
After that long drive, we are home at last.

at length—for a long time, thoroughly
We discussed that topic at length at our meeting.

at the beginning—at first, when something started
At the beginning we tried to go too fast.

at the end—when something ended
At the end of the story, everybody was happy.

at the moment—at present, now
I am very busy at the moment.

at the sound, thought, **or** prospect of—when one experiences
She gets nervous at the sound of his voice.
We shudder at the thought of moving again.
He is excited at the prospect of going to South America.

(number) at a time—ratio per instance or unit
The tall boy liked to go up the steps two or three at a time.

at once—several things together
Try to learn one step at a time, rather than three or four at once.

❺ At can mean **busy using** something; **working.**

Pattern 1: at + the + noun
I have been at the computer all day.
Nouns often used after <u>at the</u>:
cash register, computer, fax machine, ironing board, sewing machine, stove, (steering) wheel

Pattern 2: *be* + at + **work**
           be + at + **it**
You must not bother him; he is at work.
He has been at it for four hours.

Expression:
keep at it—not stop working
He wanted to go home, but he kept at it until the work was finished.

❻ At can indicate a **condition.**

Pattern: *be* + at + ø **noun**
Those two countries have been at peace for ten years.
Nouns used after at:
attention, ease, peace, rest, risk, war

Expression:
sick at heart—sad
We were sick at heart when the dog died.

❼ At can indicate **reaction.**

Pattern 1: adjective of state + at + noun
We were shocked at the condition of the classrooms.
Typical adjectives used before at:
aghast, amazed, astonished, astounded, indignant, shocked, speechless, surprised, thrilled, upset

Pattern 2: verb + at + noun
The crowd rejoiced at the good news.
Verbs commonly used before at:
cheer, grumble, guess, hint, hoot, laugh, rebel, rejoice, snort, tremble

❽ At indicates a **degree of skill.**

Pattern 1: adjective + at + noun
Your son is good at tennis, but not very good at hockey.

Pattern 2: adjective + at + verb in gerund form
That couple is really great at dancing the tango.
Typical adjectives used before at:
bad, excellent, good, great, lousy, skilled, terrible

Expression:
be an old hand at—be very experienced with
Our professor is an old hand at government operations.

⑨ At can indicate a **rate** or **level**

Pattern 1: at + noun indicating price
At the market they are selling apples at sixty-nine cents a pound.
I wish we could buy mangoes at that price.
Her husband tries to buy everything at a discount.

Pattern 2: @* + number + a + noun indicating a unit of measurement
They are selling apples @ 69¢ a lb.

Pattern 3: at + noun indicating level of age or distance
You shouldn't work so hard at your age.
He was still singing at (the age of) eighty.
We can't see very well at this distance.
The plane was flying at three thousand feet.

Expressions:
at a distance—from far away
   I saw the new baby at a distance, and he looked beautiful.

at arm's length—not close
   I try to stay at arm's length from him to avoid an argument.

Pattern 4: at + noun indicating level of speed
She shouldn't drive at that speed.
At twenty-five miles an hour on the freeway, she should get a ticket.

Exception: When speed is expressed in numbers after a verb, at is omitted.
That driver is going eighty miles an hour.
He drove sixty miles an hour the whole way home.

⑩ At can indicate the highest possible **degree** in value.

Pattern: at + superlative adjective used as noun
At best she is an adequate typist.
At least she comes to work every day.
You should be here by five o'clock at the latest.

Superlatives commonly used with this pattern:
best, least, most, worst
the earliest, the latest

⑪ Expressions
be at an advantage—be in a better-than-average position
   He is at an advantage because his family has influence.

be at a disadvantage—be in a less-than-average position
   When you are a newcomer at work, you are at a disadvantage.

---

*@ is pronounced "at." This meaning and the one for an e-mail address (section 11.1) are the only acceptable uses of this symbol.

down at the heels—shabby
His brother looked down at the heels when he was without work.

at one's mercy—in someone else's power
I was at the intruder's mercy because he had a gun in my back.

at one's discretion—someone's own decision
We can go home when we are ready, at our own discretion.

at that—
1. at that point, not any more or further
   You did a good job; leave it at that.
2. illogically
   We got lost, and in our hometown at that!

be getting at—meaning, but not saying
The manager didn't exactly say his employer had been dishonest, but we all knew what he was getting at.

⑫ Phrasal verb

pick at something (nonseparable)—try to remove something with one's fingernails
The child picked at the scab on his knee.

❶ Back to indicates **return.**

Pattern 1: verb + back to + noun of place or time
Please go back to the beginning of your story.
The children went back to the museum to see the new exhibit.
Verbs often used before <u>back to</u>:
  crawl, drive, fly, go, hark, jump, look, move, race, run, think, walk

Pattern 2: verb + noun + back to + noun
We took the train back to the city.
Typical verbs:
  bring, carry, drive, push, pull, take

❷ Back from indicates **return to a starting place from a different place.**

Pattern: verb + back from + noun of place
I'll be back (home) from the store in about ten minutes.
We can't leave until your mother gets back from her trip.
Typical verbs before <u>back from</u>:
  be, come, drive, fly, get, move, run, walk

❸ Back indicates a **return of something.**

Pattern 1: verb + noun + back (+ to + noun)
Please give this plate back to your mother.
I took the dress back to the store because it didn't fit.
Typical verbs:
  bring, give, pay, send, take

Pattern 2: verb + noun + back (+ from + noun)
Please get my suit back from the cleaners.

Pattern 3: verb + noun + back (adverb)
I called you back when I got home.
Typical verbs:
  call, bring, pay, put, take

❹ Phrasal verbs
  get back (intransitive)—move out of the way
    We wanted to see the action, but they made us get back.
  get back to someone (nonseparable)—call someone with new information
    As soon as I know the figures, I will get back to you.
  get back at someone (nonseparable)—do harm in return for a wrong
    After he was fired, he tried to get back at his boss.

get someone back (separable)—do harm in return for a wrong
  He hurt my feelings, but I got him back by hanging up the phone.
cut back (intransitive)—spend less
  With a lower salary he had to cut back.
cut back on (nonseparable)—spend less on something
  With a lower salary he had to cut back on entertainment.

1 **Before** means **earlier than.**
We must leave before four o'clock.

2 **Before** can mean **in a more important position than.**
She is so ambitious that she puts her job before her family.

3 **Before** can mean **facing.**
The handsome singer had many adoring fans before him.

4 **Before** can mean **in the future.**
The bride smiled as she thought of the happiness before her.

5 **Before** can mean **in the presence of.**
I was told to appear before the judge.

14 · BEHIND

① **Behind** means **in the rear of.**

> *The trash can is behind the chair.*
> *My friend sits behind me in class.*

② **Behind** can mean **less advanced than.**

> *Miss Thompson's class is studying lesson three; the other classes are studying lesson four. Miss Thompson's class is behind the other classes.*

③ **Behind** can mean **left in the past.**

> *He is rich now; all his financial problems are behind him.*

④ **Behind** can mean **late.**

Expressions:

1. behind schedule—later than usual
   > *The train is behind schedule.*
2. behind in payments—late in making a regular payment
   > *She is always behind in her rent payments.*

⑤ **Behind** can mean **encouraging** or **supporting.**

Pattern: noun + behind + noun

> *The successful man had an ambitious woman behind him.*
> *Those candidates have a lot of money behind them.*
> *There must be a greedy person behind this scheme.*

Typical nouns after <u>behind</u>:

a person or people
idea, plan, plot, project, scheme

⑥ Expressions

behind the scenes—not seen
> *The lawyer knew all the facts about the case; he had a lot of help behind the scenes.*

behind the times—old-fashioned
> *Her dad still uses a typewriter; he is really behind the times.*

❶ Below means **lower in number or degree than.**

Your body temperature is ninety-seven degrees; it is below normal, which is ninety-eight point six.

❷ Below can mean **lower in rank or level than.**

In our company the supervisors are below the directors.
Our offices are on the fourth floor; theirs are below ours, on the third floor.

❸ Below can mean **farther along than.**

There is a picnic ground just below the bridge.

❹ Expression

below the belt—unfairly, not according to the rules

He pretended to be her friend, then applied for her job. That was really below the belt.

16 · BENEATH

❶ Beneath means **under** and **concealed by.**

My glasses were beneath the newspaper.
The daffodils sprouted beneath the snow.

❷ Beneath can mean **less worthy than.**

Now that she is rich and famous, she thinks her family is beneath her.

❸ Beneath can mean **unlikely, because of goodness or pride.**

Pattern 1: it + *be* + beneath + noun of person + infinitive

She was a little wild, but it was beneath her to commit a crime.

Typical verbs after <u>beneath</u>:

break the law, commit adultery, commit a crime, commit perjury, gossip, lie, murder, steal

Pattern 2: noun/gerund form of verb + *be* + beneath + person

She was a little wild, but committing a crime was beneath her.

Typical nouns before <u>be beneath</u>:

adultery, breaking the law, committing a crime, forgery, lying, murder, stealing

1 Beside means **next to.**

Pattern: verb + beside + noun
Please come over here and sit beside me.
Verbs commonly used with this pattern:
be, kneel, lie (down), rest, sit (down), sleep, stand, walk, work

2 Expressions

beside the point—irrelevant
He always wastes time at our meetings by talking about things that are beside the point.
beside oneself—extremely agitated
My mother is beside herself because she doesn't know where my brother is.

18 · BESIDES

① **Besides** means **excepting.**

Everyone besides me is at the beach.

② **Besides** means **in addition to.**

Besides all of my friends, all of their brothers and sisters are there, too.

① **Between** indicates **separation of two things.**

Pattern: noun + between + noun
My neighbor and I built a fence between our backyards.

② **Between** can show **connection of two places.**
Route 395 goes between New York and Washington.

③ **Between** can indicate **a choice of.**

Pattern: verb + between + noun + and + noun
You can have only one dessert, so please decide between cake and ice cream.
Verbs often used before between:
choose, decide, judge, pick, select

④ **Between** means **not lower or higher in number.**
We have saved between three and four thousand dollars.
It is hot today. It must be between eighty and eighty-five degrees.

⑤ **Between** means **from a time to another time.**
She will be away all weekend, so don't call her between Friday night and Monday morning.

⑥ **Between** can mean **shared by.**
We are on a diet, so we will have one piece of cake between us.
They only had five dollars between them.

⑦ **Between** can mean **together.**
The newlyweds painted their new house between them.

⑧ **Expressions**

between you and me—confidentially
I don't like to spread gossip, but between you and me, they got married last week.

in between (adverb)—between, but not followed by an object.
He isn't old or young; he is in between.

20 · BEYOND

❶ Beyond means **on the other side of.**
> *Our street is beyond the traffic light.*
> *If you are traveling west, New Mexico is beyond Texas.*

❷ Beyond means **past the limits of.**

Pattern 1: *be* + beyond + noun
> *The sick child was beyond help.*
> *That situation is beyond my understanding.*

Expression:

> beyond one—not understandable by someone
> > *This puzzle is beyond me.*
> > *That technical article was beyond him.*

Pattern 2: *be* + adjective + beyond + noun
> *The palace was beautiful beyond description.*

Nouns commonly used after <u>beyond</u>:
> **belief, comprehension, help, salvation, saving, understanding, one's wildest dreams**

❸ Beyond can mean **later than.**

Pattern: beyond + noun
> *The guests were having so much fun that they stayed well beyond midnight.*
> *In this town nothing is open beyond ten o'clock.*

❹ Expressions

> beyond the pale—totally unacceptable
> > *His rude jokes at that formal reception were beyond the pale.*
>
> the great beyond (adverb)—heaven
> > *She said there would be perfect peace in the great beyond.*

1 **But** means **except.**
She works every day but Friday.

22 · BY

① By indicates an **actor, instrument,** or **cause**

Pattern: be + past participle + by + noun
The work was done by a carpenter.
The mark was made by a hammer.
The damage was caused by the storm.

② By means **following the boundary of something; along**
They walked by the side of the road.

③ By indicates a **method** or **way.**

Pattern: verb + (noun) + by + noun
She made a little money by begging.
We sent the letter by air mail.
They went to the mountains by Route 66.

④ By can mean **according to** a form, period of time, packaging, weight, number, or amount

Pattern: verb + (noun) + by + the + noun
He makes his decisions by the rules.
She charges by the hour.
We buy eggs by the dozen.
Typical nouns after <u>by the</u>:
  day, hour, month, week
  job, piece
  bag, barrel, box, bucket, bushel, cup, drop, gallon, ounce, pint, pound, quart, ream, tablespoonful, teaspoonful

⑤ By can mean **not later than.**
You must be here by six A.M. sharp.
I'm worried; they should have arrived by now.

Expression:
  by the time—when
    By the time you get up, I'll be in New York.

⑥ By means **near** or **next to.**
His desk is by mine.
I hope you will stay by me.

⑦ By indicates **multiplication, division,** and **square measurement.**
We multiplied four by three. (4 × 3 = 12)
They divided ten by two. (10 ÷ 2 = 5)
That room measures ten feet by twelve feet. It measures 120 square feet.

❽ By can mean **a lot of.**

Pattern: by + the + noun
   He gets letters by the hundreds every day.
Typical nouns used after <u>by the</u>:
   dozens, hundreds, thousands, truckload

❾ By can indicate **the extent of a win or a loss.**
   That horse won by a nose.
   They lost the basketball game by three points.

Expressions:

   by a mile—by a lot; to a great extent
      We won the game by a mile.

   by far—without question
      He is by far the strongest man here.

❿ Expressions

   by all means—certainly
      You should by all means visit the art gallery.
   (all) by oneself—alone; without help
      The children are at home by themselves.
      The girl made the cake all by herself.
   by day—during the day; by night—during the night
      Most people work by day and sleep by night.
   by chance—for no apparent reason
      I saw my teacher at the mall by chance.
   by (any) chance—perhaps
      Do you by any chance have change for a dollar?
   by the way—incidentally
      By the way, my aunt is coming to visit next week. Why don't you come see her?
   little by little (adverb)—slowly
      He practiced every day, and little by little, began to show improvement.
   one by one—one at a time; two by two—two at a time
      One by one, she picked up the pearls from her broken necklace.
      The schoolchildren walked to the museum, two by two, holding hands.
   by profession—indicates one's job
      He is a teacher by profession.
   by nature/by disposition—naturally
      She is generous by nature.
      He is nervous by disposition.
   by reputation—indicates common belief
      She is a good lawyer by reputation.
   go by the board—be ignored
      Our suggestions for improving the company went by the board.

by and by (adverb)—one day, in the future
We'll meet again, by and by.

by and large (adverb)—almost completely
The company is doing well, by and large.

⑪ Phrasal verbs

do well by (nonseparable)—be responsible for someone's benefit
She was a good mother; she did well by her children.

stand by (nonseparable)—to support
She stood by me when I was in trouble.

swear by (nonseparable)—have complete faith in the worth of something
My mother swears by that cleaning product.

drop by (intransitive)—visit without notice
Your friends dropped by this afternoon, but you weren't here.

drop by (separable)—to deliver
A boy dropped this package by today.

get by (intransitive)—live, but with difficulty
He's feeble, but he gets by.

go by (nonseparable)—pass in front of
We went by your house last night.

put by (separable)—store
She put her dreams by for a while.

run by (separable)—to tell in detail
She ran her story by me several times this afternoon.

1 **Close to** means **near.**
> *Your house is close to the metro station.*
> *They are sitting close to each other.*

2 **Close to** indicates **a very friendly** or **intimate relationship.**
> *She is very close to her older sister.*

3 **Close to** (adverb) can mean **almost.**
> *I wrote close to fifty invitations this morning.*

❶ Despite indicates **an illogical occurrence.**
   We had a good time despite the bad weather.

❷ In spite of has the same meaning and usage as despite.
   We had a good time in spite of the bad weather.

❶ Down indicates **movement from a higher place.**

Pattern: noun + verb + down + noun
The rocks rolled down the mountain.
Typical verbs used before <u>down</u>:
come, fall, go, move, roll, run, slide, walk

❷ Down means **following the way of; along**

Pattern 1: noun + verb + down + noun
The old man went down the road on foot.
Typical verbs used before <u>down</u>:
come, drive, go, move, run, skate, walk

Pattern 2: noun + verb + noun + down + noun
The boys rode their bikes down the street this morning.
Typical verbs before <u>down</u>:
bring, carry, drive, move, pull, push, ride, take
Typical nouns after <u>down</u>:
freeway, highway, path, road, sidewalk, street, turnpike

❸ Down indicates **destruction.**

Pattern 1: noun + verb + down + noun
The intruder broke down the door.
Typical verbs used before <u>down</u>:
blow, break, bring, burn, cut, strike, take

Pattern 2: verb + noun + down
The intruder broke the door down.

❹ Expression
upside down—turned so that the bottom is on top
The cups go in the dishwasher upside down.

❺ Phrasal verbs
back down (intransitive)—retreat
The dog backed down when I called his name.

calm down (separable)—soothe; tranquilize
We had to calm the children down after the excitement.

close down (separable)—stop business activity, temporarily or permanently
We close the shop down at four o'clock every day.
They plan to close that business down for good.

come down with (nonseparable)—become sick
She missed the picnic because she came down with the flu.

crack down on (nonseparable)—impose restrictions
The police are cracking down on street violence.

let down (separable)—disappoint
She let me down when she didn't help me with my party.

look down on (nonseparable)—feel superior to
The older students tend to look down on the younger ones.

mark down (separable)—lower in price
I bought this shirt after they marked it down to ten dollars.

put down (separable)—insult
She shouldn't go out with him; he puts her down all the time.

run down (separable)—criticize negatively
She always runs her hometown down.

shut down (separable)—turn off a computer; end a business
She worked all night and didn't shut her computer down until morning.
They shut that shop down two years ago.

turn down (separable)—reject
He got a job offer today but he is going to turn it down.

write down (separable)—put on paper for future reference
She didn't know my phone number, so I wrote it down for her.

1 **During** indicates **within a period of time.**
We slept during the day.
They practiced basketball during the summer.

2 **During** means **at the same time as another event.**
I slept during the football game.
They lived in the north during the war.

① **Except** means **excluding.**

Everyone went to the movies except me.
We work every day except Sunday.

❶ Far (away) from indicates **a great distance between places or people.**
> *Their office isn't far (away) from here.*
> *His sister moved far from home a long time ago.*

❷ Far from (adverb) can mean **not.**

Pattern: far from + adjective
> *His wife is far from perfect.*

Adjectives often used with this pattern:
> **ideal, perfect, wonderful**

29 · FOR

① For indicates a **recipient** or **beneficiary**.

Pattern 1: noun + for + noun
I have a present for you.
Nouns often used before for:
answer, cure, gift, idea, job, message, letter, plan, present, project, question, suggestion, surprise, secret

Pattern 2: noun + for + ø noun
We have news for you.
Typical nouns before for:
advice, help, information, news, nothing, something

Pattern 3: verb + noun + for + noun
She sang a song for me.
He only wants the best for you.
Verbs often used before for:
bake, build, buy, care, cook, create, dance, design, do, get, make, perform, play, sing, want, win, work, write

② For indicates **a special purpose.**

Pattern 1: noun + for + noun
You need a coat for winter.
He has a bicycle for transportation.

Pattern 2: noun + for + verb in gerund form
They have a special place for washing cars.
The doctor has a machine for measuring blood pressure.

Expression:
room for—enough space for something or somebody
We need room for twenty people for our party.
We don't have room for a grand piano.

③ For can indicate the **intended result** of an action.

Pattern 1: verb + for + noun
The boys were screaming for help.
What are you looking for?
Verbs often used before for:
apply, ask, audition, beg, call, campaign, compete, cry, fight, go out, go, hope, long, look, petition, plead, pray, register, run, scream, send, shop, shout, stand in line, strive, study, train, try out, wait, whistle, wish, work, yell

Expression:
run for office—be a candidate in an election
After he ran for president and lost, he said he would never run for office again.

Pattern 2: verb + someone + for + noun
We nominated him for president of the club.
Typical verbs:
ask, need, nominate, send, train, want

Pattern 3: noun + for + noun
I hope they are developing a cure for the flu.
Do you have a good recipe for lemon pie?
Nouns often used before <u>for</u>:
cure, directions, idea, instructions, lesson, need, pattern, plan, program, project, recipe, system

Pattern 4: *be* + adjective of condition + for + noun
I am hungry for steak and french fries.
They are ready for the ball game.
Adjectives often used before <u>for</u>:
anxious, eager, greedy, hungry, impatient, prepared, ready, starved, thirsty

❹ For can explain the **reason** of an action or fact.

Pattern 1: verb + for + noun
He apologized for his absence.

Pattern 2: verb + for + gerund form of verb
He apologized for arriving late.

Pattern 3: verb + someone + for + noun
They rewarded her for bravery.
They congratulated him for graduating.
Verbs often used before <u>for</u>:
book, chide, cite, compensate, congratulate, criticize, expel, fine, get, honor, pay, praise, punish, reimburse, reprimand, reward, scold, tease

Pattern 4: *be* + adjective + for + noun
She is famous for her great parties.
She is famous for giving great parties.
Adjectives often used before <u>for</u>:
famous, feared, known, notorious, popular, loved, well-known

❺ For can indicate the **expected benefit** of an action.

Pattern: verb + for + noun
We play soccer for fun.
Typical nouns after <u>for</u>:
exercise, fun, happiness, kicks, money, peace, pleasure, practice, relaxation, security

6 For can indicate the **effect** of an adjective.

Pattern 1: *be* + adjective + for + noun
Calcium is good for your bones and teeth.
Adjectives often used before for:
   accessible, available, bad, crucial, good, healthy, helpful, important, necessary, unhealthy, useful

Pattern 2: It + *be* + adjective + for + object + infinitive
It was hard for him to make good grades.
Adjectives often used before for:
   bad, better, challenging, customary, crucial, good, helpful, important, impossible, necessary, possible, ridiculous, unimportant, unnecessary, unusual, usual, useful, useless, wasteful, worse

Pattern 3: *be* + (not) adjective + enough + for + noun
This apartment is good enough for me.

Pattern 4: *be* + too + adjective + for + noun
That course was too hard for him.
This apartment is too small for three people.

7 For can indicate the **recipient** of someone's feelings.

Pattern: *be* + adjective + for + noun (person)
We are happy for her on her wedding day.
Why are you sorry for yourself?
Typical adjectives before for:
   delighted, happy, pleased, sorry, thrilled

8 For can indicate activity or preparation on an **occasion.**

Pattern: verb + (noun) + for + noun
What do you want for your birthday?
What did you have for dinner?
Typical nouns after for:
   one's anniversary, birthday, graduation
   breakfast, dinner, the holidays, lunch

9 For indicates **a substitute.**

Pattern 1: noun + for + noun
We had to use a newspaper for an umbrella.
I'm sorry, I mistook you for someone else.

Pattern 2: verb + for + noun
He taught the class for our teacher, who was sick.
Verbs often used with this meaning:
   act, conduct, direct, drive, fill in, operate, manage, run, speak, stand in, substitute, teach, work

⑩ For can mean **available.**

Pattern: noun + for + noun
The house is for sale.
The pianos are for use by the students.
Nouns often used after for:
   hire, practice, purchase, rent, sale, use

Expression:
   up for grabs—available to many people
    The chairmanship is up for grabs.

⑪ For can indicate a **destination.**

Pattern: verb + for + noun
We are leaving for Spain in two weeks.
Verbs used before for:
   head, leave, plan, set out, start out, take off

⑫ For can indicate **representation.**
Red is for stop; yellow is for caution; green is for go.
M is for Mary.

⑬ For can indicate **equality in an exchange.**

Pattern 1: *be* **+ noun + for + noun**
The bananas are two pounds for a dollar.

Pattern 2: verb + noun + for + noun
We bought three books for twenty-five dollars.
Typical verbs:
   buy, do, exchange, hand over, make, rent, sell, take, trade, want

Pattern 3: verb + for + noun
He works for twenty dollars an hour.

Expression:
   for free—without charge
   for nothing — without charge

⑭ For can indicate **amount.**

Pattern: noun + for + noun
The mechanic sent them a bill for three hundred dollars.
Nouns often used before for:
   bill, check, invoice, receipt, request

⑮ For can indicate **length of time.**
He was here for ten years.

Expressions:

for good—forever
He came to live in this country for good.

for life—until death
They sent him to prison for life.

⑯ For can indicate **need on a future date.**
She needs the musicians for Thursday afternoon.

⑰ For can mean **despite.**

Pattern: for + all + possessive pronoun + noun
For all her experience, she's not a very good secretary.
Nouns often used with this meaning:
education, experience, expertise, knowledge, popularity, qualifications, training

⑱ For indicates the **person or people responsible for an action.**

Pattern: for + person + infinitive
Your final grade is for the teacher to decide.
That problem is for you to solve.

⑲ For can describe a **sense** or **talent.**

Pattern: *have* + noun + for + noun
He has an ear for music.
She has a touch for the piano.
Nouns often used before for:
aptitude, ear, eye, knack, rhythm, talent, touch, voice

Expressions with this meaning:

have a nose for gossip—often hear and spread news about others
have an eye for the girls—often admire pretty women

⑳ For can indicate an **unusual fact.**

Pattern 1: adjective + for + noun
That boy is tall for his age.
It's warm for February.

Pattern 2: adverb + for + noun
She plays very well for a beginner.

㉑ For can indicate **favor** or **support.**

Pattern: verb + for + noun
We are for higher wages.
You have to stand up for your rights.
Verbs often used before for:
be, cheer, push, show respect, stand, stand up

Expression:
to have a preference for—to prefer
She has a preference for the other job.

㉒ For can mean **because of.**
We are thankful for your help.
She is grateful for her family.
For as a conjunction means **because.**
She went home early, for she was sick.

㉓ Expressions

for once—for the first time, showing exasperation
Would you please be at work on time for once!

once and for all—immediately and forever after
She decided to stop smoking once and for all.

word for word—reading or talking slowly, one word at a time
He read the letter to me word for word.

for the time being—meanwhile; until something happens to change the situation
We can't do anything now, so for the time being we will act as usual.

for fear of—in order to avoid
He worked and saved for fear of being poor again.

for a change—as usual, sarcastically
It's raining for a change.

be for the best—even though the situation is unpleasant, it may be good.
I was sad when she died, but it was for the best, because she was suffering a lot.

go for a drive/run/swim/walk—spend a short time doing that activity
We always go for a walk after lunch.

see for oneself—investigate personally
I couldn't believe her, so I decided to see for myself.

for better or for worse—accepting all conditions, regardless of what happens in the future
He promised to stay with her forever, for better or for worse.

for naught—with no result
Our efforts were all for naught; we lost.

㉔ Phrasal verbs

go (in) for (nonseparable)—like a lot
The college girls really go for Latin dancing.

go out for (nonseparable)—audition or perform for selection
She went out for the softball team, but she didn't make it.

care for (nonseparable)—love
She really cares for him.

care for (nonseparable)—want
She doesn't care for more ice cream, thank you.

fall for (nonseparable)—innocently believe or trust
He falls for all of her tricks.

not stand for (nonseparable)—not allow
The teacher won't stand for talking during a test.

stand up for (nonseparable)—support publicly
His best friend stood up for him through all his problems.

take for (separable)—consider as
Don't take him for a fool; he is really quite smart.

❶ From indicates a **source.**

Pattern 1: verb + from + noun
Tony is from Alabama.
I hear from him every week.
Verbs commonly used before from:
 be, call, come, derive, hear

Pattern 2: verb + noun + from + noun
We get help from our neighbors.
Verbs commonly used with this pattern:
 borrow, bring, buy, collect, copy, get, mail, obtain, receive, send

❷ From indicates a **point of departure.**

Pattern: verb + from + noun (place)
The ship sailed from San Francisco.
Please start from the beginning.
Typical verbs:
 begin, depart, drive, fly, go, graduate, move, read, sail, start (over), take off

❸ From can indicate **separation.**

Pattern 1: verb + away + from + noun
We ran away from the building.
Keep away from the crowd.
Typical verbs before away from:
 drive, get, keep, move, run, walk

Pattern 2: verb + noun + from + noun
We collected the papers from the students.
Verbs commonly used with this pattern:
 borrow, buy, chase, collect, delete, dissociate, eliminate, erase, expel, hide,
 keep (away), protect, release, remove, save, scare (away), separate, shield,
 steal, subtract, take (away)

❹ From can indicate **difference.**

Pattern 1: number + from + number
Three from nine equals six.

Pattern 2: number + noun of time or distance + from
He lives five miles from here.
They are only twenty minutes (away) from the city.
I will see you two weeks from today.
Expressions:
 be different from
  My sweater is different from yours.

differ from
   My opinion differs from his.

distinguish from—identify in a comparison
   I can't distinguish her from her twin sister.

tell from—identify in a comparison
   I can't tell her from her twin sister.

know from—identify in a comparison
   I don't know her from her twin sister.

⑤ From . . . to can indicate the lowest and highest limits of an estimate; **between.**

Pattern: from + number + to + number
   You will earn from ten to fifteen dollars an hour.
   We expect from twenty-five to thirty people.

⑥ From . . . to can give the **starting and ending time or place.**
   We work from nine A.M. to five P.M.
Common expressions with this meaning:
   from beginning to end
   from front to back
   from May to September
   from one place to another
   from one side to the other
   from start to finish
   from top to bottom

⑦ From can indicate the **material** something is composed of.

Pattern: *be* + past participle of verb + from + noun
   This suit was made from three different fabrics.
   A new plant has been developed from those seeds.
Past participles commonly used before from:
   crafted, created, derived, developed, fashioned, made, put together, sewn

⑧ From can indicate a **position** for viewing or hearing.
   I can see the bridge from my window.
   Let's try to see the problem from his point of view.
   Can you hear the actors from the back of the auditorium?
Expressions commonly used with this meaning:
   here, there
   my/your/his/her/our/their point of view
   this/that angle, position, vantage point, distance

⑨ From can indicate a **result.**

Pattern 1: adjective + from + gerund form of verb
They are exhausted from working so hard.
Adjectives often used with this pattern:
better, bored, drunk, exhausted, healthy, fat, sick, sore, tired, well, worse

Pattern 2: verb + noun + from + noun
They knew the songs from memory.
He learned his lesson from hard work.
Typical nouns after from:
listening, memory, hard work, studying

Expression:

to suffer from—to hurt because of
She suffers from neglect.

⑩ From can indicate **avoidance.**

Pattern 1: verb + from + noun
Try to keep from shaking.
We can't hide from them any longer.

Pattern 2: verb + direct object + from + verb in gerund form
Try to keep him from shaking.
They hope to stop her from running away.
Typical verbs:
keep, prevent, stop

⑪ From can mean **because of.**

Pattern: from + noun
From the way he walks, I think his ankle is sprained.
From his accent, I believe he is from Boston.

❶ In indicates **location inside** or **within** something else.

Pattern 1: verb + in + noun
We live in that house.
The pencils are in the box.

Nouns commonly used after in:
Geographical areas:
city, continent, country, state, town
He lives in Seattle, Washington, in the U.S.A.
Comfortable, protected places:
alcove, large chair, cocoon, nest
He sat down in the chair and read his novel.
Inside areas:
attic, balcony, basement, building, corner, hall, kitchen, office, room
She is in her office, in that building, in room 302, in the corner.
Vehicles where the passengers cannot walk around:
car, canoe, helicopter, small airplane, small boat
We went in the car, but they went in a helicopter.
Publications and speeches
article, book, dictionary, encyclopedia, lecture, magazine, newspaper, speech
He didn't say that in his speech, but I read it in the newspaper.

Pattern 2: *be* + in + ø noun
He can't come to the phone because he's in bed.

Nouns commonly used after in:
bed, church, class, jail, place, school, town

Pattern 3: verb + noun + in + noun
Put the pencils in the box.

Typical verbs:
drop, get, insert, lay, place, push, put
Typical nouns:
bag, box, drawer, file, folder, notebook, sack, suitcase, trunk, wallet

❷ In indicates **membership** of a group or category.

Pattern: *be* + noun + in + noun
There are seven people in our family.
Your brother is the expert in that office.

Nouns commonly used after in:
association, category, choir, chorus, club, family, fraternity, group, office, society, sorority

❸ In can indicate a **period of time.**

Pattern: *be* + in + time period
century
in + the   *She was born in the 1800s.*

decade in + the	*He lived in Arkansas in the 1950s.* *Life was quieter in the fifties.*
month in + ø	*He took his vacation in March.*
period of the day in + the	*I work in the morning.* *My boss works in the afternoon.* *We relax in the evening.*
period of time in general in + the	*We lived there in the past, and we will live here in the future.*
stage of life in + ø	**adulthood, childhood, death, health, life, sickness** In childhood she was always in good health.
season in + (ø)	**spring, summer, fall, winter** They always go to Europe in (the) summer.
year in + ø	Their son was born in 1994.
during general activities in + one's	**actions, deeds, dreams, prayers, thoughts** She is always in our thoughts.

Expression:

in advance—before an event
To get tickets to the concert, you have to pay in advance.

❹ In can mean **after** a period of **time.**

Pattern: in + (number) + noun
She will be here in five minutes.

Expression:

in no time—very soon
He will be here in no time.

❺ In can mean **movement** or **transfer** from one place into another.

Pattern 1: verb + in(to) + noun
They went in the store.
Verbs often used with this meaning:
   burst, butt, come, go, get, jump, move, run, walk

Pattern 2: verb + noun + in + noun
Please pour the juice in the glass.
Typical verbs:
   draw, drop, fly, lay, place, pour, pull, push, put, ram, shove, squeeze, throw

Pattern 3: verb + object + in
When you finish your test, hand it in (to the teacher).
Typical verbs:
  bring, hand, pass, take, turn

6 **In** indicates the **number of individual parts** of something.

Pattern: number + plural noun + in + noun
There are seven days in a week.
There are 100 cents in a dollar.

7 **In** means during a type of **weather.**

Pattern 1: in + the + noun
They walked all day in the rain.
Nouns used with this pattern:
  cold, fog, heat, humidity, rain, snow, storm, sun

Pattern 2: in + ø + noun
In hot weather we stay inside.
Nouns used with this pattern:
  bad weather, cold weather, foggy weather, good weather, hot weather, rainy weather, sunshine

8 **In** can indicate separated **parts** of something.

Pattern: verb + noun + in(to) + plural noun
She cut the cake in twelve pieces.
Verbs commonly used with this pattern:
  cut, divide, separate, sever, split
Nouns commonly used after in:
  halves, parts, pieces, portions, sections

Expression:
in two—in halves
  We only had one candy bar, so we cut it in two and shared it.

9 **In** can indicate **direction.**
The girls came in this direction, and the boys went in the opposite direction.

Expression: (adjective, adverb)
in-bound—moving toward the city or town
  There was a lot of in-bound traffic this morning.

10 **In** can indicate **ratio.**

Pattern: number + in + number
He is one in a million.
Four in ten are employed full-time.

⑪ In indicates the **style** or **composition** of recorded material.

Pattern: in + noun
The letter was written in ink.
They printed the photographs in duplicate.
Nouns commonly used after in:
bold, black and white, capital letters, color, duplicate, ink, italics, lower case, oil, pencil, print, water colors

⑫ In indicates the use of a **language** or **style** of expression.

Pattern: in + ø noun
The paper was written in English.
The girls chorus sang in harmony.
Nouns often used after in:
a few words, chorus, code, concert, detail, full, harmony, music, poetry, rhythm, sync, tune, verse

Adverbial pattern: in + adjective
In brief, we are leaving in five minutes.
In short, everybody is getting a raise in pay.

Expression:
tongue-in-cheek—sarcastically
All the nice things he said about her were said tongue-in-cheek.

⑬ In indicates **current style.**

Pattern: in + ø noun
Her clothes are always in fashion.
She likes to be in style.
Nouns used with this pattern:
style, fashion, season, vogue

Expression:
to be "in"—to be in fashion
High-heeled shoes are in again this season.

⑭ In indicates a **condition.**

Pattern 1: *be* + in + a + noun
She is always in a good mood.
Nouns commonly used with this pattern:
hurry, mess, good/bad mood, rage, stew

Pattern 2: verb + in + ø noun
We are in good health.
She ran into the room in tears.

Nouns often used with this pattern:
> **anguish, awe, chaos, comfort, condition, confusion, danger, despair, dire straits, disarray, disaster, disgrace, disorder, doubt, dread, fear, good/bad health, love, need, pain, ruins, shape, sickness, tears, trouble**

Expressions:
> to be in hot water—to be in trouble
> *She has been late three times, and now she's really in hot water with the boss.*

> to be in the black—to be out of debt
> *We have paid off all our credit cards; we are finally in the black.*

⑮ In describes a manner of **behavior.**

Pattern 1: verb + in + a + noun
He spoke in a loud voice.
Nouns often used with this pattern:
> **manner, voice, way**

Pattern 2: verb + noun + in + ø noun
He told me that story in confidence.
Nouns often used after in:
> **cold blood, confidence, fairness, friendship, fun, person, silence, someone's absence, someone's presence, trust**

Adverbial pattern: verb + noun + in + adjective
She is working on her exams in earnest.
Typical adjectives after in:
> **earnest, private, public**

Expressions:
> in deference to—with great respect for
> *We are acting in deference to our chairman's wishes.*

> hand-in-hand (adverb)—with hands linked
> *Couples love to walk hand-in-hand.*

> arm-in-arm (adverb)—with arms linked
> *She always walked arm-in-arm with her mother.*

⑯ In means **wearing.**

Pattern 1: in + noun
She came in a long dress, and he was in a suit and tie.
Typical nouns:
> **bathing suit, coat, dress, hat, skirt, suit, tie, tee shirt**

Pattern 2: in + ø noun
Everybody went to the party in costume.
Typical nouns:
> **black (or any color), braces, braids, costume, curls, disguise, drag, high heels, jeans, jewels, make-up, mourning (black), ponytails, (tennis) shoes, shorts, uniform**

Expression:
> in the nude—not wearing anything
> > *He sleeps in the nude.*

㊵ In indicates involvement in a career or project.

Pattern: *be/be involved/work* **+ in + ø noun**
> *My uncle is in business for himself.*
> *She has worked in insurance for years.*
> *They are involved in computers.*

Nouns commonly used with this pattern:
> **accounting, administration, architecture, banking, business, computers, entertainment, government, insurance, journalism, landscaping, law, medicine, politics, publishing, research, stocks and bonds, teaching, training, the air force, the army, the coast guard, the marines, the military, the navy, the reserves**

㊶ In defines an **arrangement.**

Pattern 1: in + a + singular noun
> *The children all sat in a circle.*

Nouns often used with this meaning:
> **circle, group, line, pile, row, stack**

Pattern 2: in + plural or noncount noun
> *She put the clothes in piles on the floor.*

Nouns often used with this meaning:
> **bunches, bundles, folds, groups, lines, piles, rows, stacks**
> **alignment, order**

Expression:
> to be in line—to be waiting in an orderly fashion, one after the other

㊷ In indicates **composition of money.**

Pattern: in + noun
> *She always pays in cash.*
> *I have six dollars in change.*

Nouns used with this meaning:
> **bills, cash, change, checks, coins, dimes, dollars, nickels, pennies, quarters**
> **ones (one-dollar bills), fives, tens, twenties, fifties, hundreds**

㊸ In indicates **purpose.**

Pattern 1: in + ø noun + of + noun
> *We are here in memory of our dear brother.*
> *They came in search of gold.*

Nouns commonly used with this meaning:
> **aid, appreciation, celebration, commemoration, dedication, honor, lieu, memory, praise, search**

Expression:
> in compensation for—to restore balance, pay for
> *She made me a dress in compensation for the favors I did for her.*

Pattern 2: in + order + to + verb
She came here in order to learn English.
They are saving money in order to buy a car.

㉑ In can define a measurement.

Pattern 1: number + noun + in + noun
The box is one foot in height, eight inches in depth, and eight inches in width.

Pattern 2: verb + in + noun
We weigh in pounds; I don't know my weight in kilos.
Typical nouns used after in:
centimeters, feet, inches, kilos, meters, miles, ounces, pounds, yards

㉒ In can indicate a special relationship.

Pattern 1: in + ø noun + with + noun
All of the parents are working in cooperation with the teachers.
Nouns often used with this meaning:
agreement, alignment, cahoots, collaboration, collusion, combination, common, comparison, competition, conflict, conjunction, connection, cooperation, contact, debate, dispute, good, harmony, rhythm, step, sympathy, touch, trouble

Pattern 2: in + noun + with + noun
She was in a fight with him yesterday.
Typical nouns used before in:
argument, debate, exchange, fight, session, situation

㉓ In indicates a location on the body.

Pattern 1: verb + noun + in + the + body part
He kicked the attacker in the stomach.
She scratched herself in the eye.
Verbs commonly used with this pattern:
hit, hurt, kick, knock, poke, punch, scratch, slap, strike

Pattern 2: have + noun + in + possessive pronoun + noun
I have a pain in my chest.
She has an ache in her left leg.

Expression:
> to be a pain in the neck—to be annoying
> *Her little sister is eight years old, and she's a pain in the neck.*

㉔ In can indicate a **current state.**

Pattern 1: *be* + in + ø noun
The papers are in circulation.
Your book is in demand.
The car is not in gear

Nouns commonly used with this pattern:
bankruptcy, captivity, charge, check, circulation, confinement, conflict, control, debt, demand, jail, power, session, trouble, trust

Nouns referring to the transmission of a car or other vehicle:
drive, first, second, third, fourth, fifth, gear, neutral, park, reverse

Expressions:
in a corner—trapped
With so many bills, and no job, he was really in a corner.

in the dark—ignorant of the facts
My colleagues kept me in the dark about their plans to leave the company.

in good hands (with)—well-served
I know I am in good hands with my lawyer.

㉕ In can indicate a **reaction.**

Pattern: verb + in + ø noun
Her friend left in disgust.
She hung her head in disappointment.

Nouns commonly used after in:
apprehension, approbation, approval, assent, compliance, confusion, consent, contempt, defeat, defiance, delight, disappointment, disdain, disgrace, disgust, dismay, disobedience, dissent, desolation, grief, happiness, pain, reaction, relief, sadness, sorrow, the affirmative

Typical verbs used before in:
cry, exclaim, go away, leave, react, scream, smile, sneer, squeal, tremble, weep hang/nod/shake one's head, stick up one's nose

㉖ In can indicate **quantities.**

Pattern: in + plural noun
People came in thousands to see the shrine.

Nouns typically used after in:
busloads, carloads, groups of ten, hordes, hundreds, small groups, thousands, truckloads

㉗ In can indicate an **example.**

Pattern: noun + in + noun that names first noun
She has a good friend in Mrs. Jones.
They have a wonderful teacher in John Smith.

28 In can mean **when.**

Pattern: in + verb in gerund form
She is correct in saying that he was lazy.
In signing your name, you are admitting guilt.

29 In can refer to the **process of a game.**

Pattern: in + name of game
In baseball, there are nine players on a team.
The boys have been in a game of chess all afternoon.
Names of common games:
badminton, baseball, bridge, canasta, cards, chess, football, golf, hide-and-seek, hockey, monopoly, polo, racquetball, solitaire, tag, tennis, volleyball

30 In can mean **on the occasion of.**

Pattern: in + ø noun
She smiled in acceptance.
He nodded his head in agreement.
Nouns often used with this meaning:
acceptance, action, comparison, conclusion, contrast, conversation, defeat, practice, return, the end

31 In can indicate a **warning** or **prediction** of a reaction.

Pattern: be + in + for + a + noun
He is in for a shock when he gets here tomorrow.
Nouns used with this meaning:
rude awakening, shock, surprise, treat

32 In can define the **emphasis** or **perspective** of a statement.

Pattern 1: in + ø noun
In fact, this is a very good report.
The children behave themselves in general.
Nouns commonly used after in:
addition, all, all seriousness, analysis, answer, conclusion, fact, general, particular, question, return, reverse, theory, truth

Pattern 2: in + one's + noun
In my opinion, this is a mistake.
Typical nouns:
case, heart, opinion, view

Expressions:
in any case—no matter what happens
We will have the party in any case.

in that case—if that happens
In that case, everybody will stay at home.

Pattern 3: in + the + noun
In the end, everything was fine.
Nouns used with this pattern:
  end, final analysis

Pattern 4: in + noun + of + noun
She went to the party in spite of her mother's wishes.
In case of fire, leave the building.
Nouns used with this pattern:
  case, light, spite, terms, view

33 **In** can indicate the **quality** of a noun.

Pattern 1: *be* + adjective + in + noun
They are lacking in the necessities of a decent life.
Those people may be poor in commodities, but they are rich in spirit.
Her sister is blind in one eye.

Pattern 2: *be* + the + superlative adjective + noun + in + name of category
He is the best student in the class.
That is the longest river in the world.

34 **In** can indicate a **topic.**

Pattern 1: noun + in + noun
There was a big improvement in her grades this term.
Typical nouns before in:
  advance, change, decline, decrease, improvement, increase

Pattern 2: verb + in + noun
She participated in the planning of the conference.
He persists in calling me on the telephone.
Typical verbs:
  assist, cooperate, help, invest, participate, persist

Pattern 3: adjective + in + noun
This land is rich in minerals.
She is very interested in antique furniture.
Typical adjectives:
  basking, covered, drowning, interested, rich, steeped, submerged

35 **Expressions**
in addition to—plus
  In addition to your car payment, you will have to pay for registration and insurance.
in the air—an indication that something has been discussed
  A raise in salaries is in the air.

in sight—an indication that something is visible, or will happen soon
We are almost there; the bridge is in sight.
The work is almost finished; our vacation is in sight.

㊱ Phrasal verbs

break in (intransitive)—enter without permission, removing a barrier
Someone broke in yesterday and took their bicycles.

break in on (nonseparable)—enter without permission, surprising those inside
We were having a private conversation when he broke in on us.

break in (separable)—use something for first time, as a warm-up; to tame
The boy got a new bicycle and couldn't wait to break it in.

butt in (intransitive)—interrupt a private conversation
Everything was fine until she butted in.

check in (intransitive)—register
After they checked in at the desk they went to their room.

check in (separable)—leave something temporarily in a guarded place
The bags were heavy, so he checked them in right away.

chip in (intransitive)—contribute
The students all chipped in and bought the teacher a present.

close in (on) (nonseparable)—approach and surround
The people were scared as the enemy closed in on them.

count in (separable)—expect someone's participation
If you are looking for volunteers, count me in.

do in (separable)—tire
I exercised at the gym for two hours, and it did me in.

drop in (separable)—let something fall into a deep container
After you finish the letter, please drop it in the mailbox.

drop in (on) (nonseparable)—visit someone without notice
We hadn't seen them in years, and they dropped in on us yesterday morning.

fill in (separable)—complete a form
Here is the application form; please fill it in.

fill in (for) (nonseparable)—substitute
Another doctor is filling in for her while she's on vacation.

get in (nonseparable)—enter, perhaps with slight difficulty
The door was locked, but we got in through the window.

get in (separable)—place inside, perhaps with slight difficulty
The mailslot was too small for the package; I couldn't get it in.

give in (to) (nonseparable)—surrender
I hope she never gives in to his wishes; he wants to control her.

keep in (separable)—not allow to go out
The child was sick and his mother kept him in.

key in (separable)—type into the computer
First you have to key in your password.

kick in (intransitive)—contribute
When it gets very cold, the electric heater kicks in.

look in (on) (nonseparable)—occasionally check
Will you look in on my mother every afternoon while I'm away?

step in (intransitive)—enter
I knocked on the door and he told me to step in.

squeeze in (separable)—make room or time for somebody
The doctor was busy, but he managed to squeeze me in.

turn in (intransitive)—go to bed
They were really tired, and had to turn in.

take in (separable)—to make smaller
The skirt was too big, so she took it in at the waist.

take in (separable)—to comprehend
I'm not sure she took in everything you were saying.

❶ In back of means located **behind.**

Pattern 1: noun + in back of + noun
There is a beautiful tree in back of our house.

Pattern 2: verb + in back of + noun
Your sister sits in back of me in class.

1 **In front of** means located **before** or **facing** something.

Pattern 1: noun + in front of + noun
There is a van in front of their house.

Pattern 2: verb + in front of + noun
The teacher usually stands in front of the class.
He was in front of me in line.

2 **In front of** can mean **in the future.**
She has a lot of problems in front of her.

34 · INSIDE

1 **Inside** means **within** something else.

Pattern: verb + noun + inside + noun
There are some little toy animals inside the box.
She put the money inside the envelope.

2 **Inside** (adverb) means **indoors,** within a building.
It started to rain, so we went inside.

① **Instead of** means **substituting for.**

Pattern: verb + noun + instead of + noun
They went to Hawaii instead of South America.
She cooks a lot of vegetables instead of meat.

❶ Into indicates **entrance.**

Pattern 1: verb + into + noun
We went into his office.
I drive into the city every day.
Typical verbs before into:
blow, break, come, drive, fall, fly, gaze, get, go, look, move, walk, run, sail, stare, stomp, storm

Pattern 2: verb + noun + into + noun
She poured the juice into the glass.
Verbs often used with this pattern:
blow, cram, drive, get, move, place, pour, put, set, throw

❷ Into can indicate **forced contact.**

Pattern: verb + into + noun
That car crashed into a tree.
Verbs often used before into:
crash, push, pull, run, smash, tear

Expression:

to run something into the ground—to talk about something too much
We are sick of hearing about his job; he really runs it into the ground.

❸ Into can indicate **division.**

Pattern 1: number + into + number = number
Three into twelve equals four.

Pattern 2: verb + noun + into + (number) + noun
She cut the pie into eight wedges.
The vase broke into a million pieces.
Typical verbs before into:
arrange, break, cut, divide, separate
Typical nouns after into:
bits, parts, pieces, slices, wedges

❹ Into can indicate a **change in condition or form.**

Pattern 1: *go/get* **+ into + ø noun**
They went into debt after the accident.
He always gets into trouble at school.
Nouns often used after go into:
action, bankruptcy, debt
Nouns used after get into:
danger, condition, shape, trouble

Pattern 2: *go/get* + into + noun
> *He went into a rage.*
> *They got into an argument.*

Typical nouns after <u>go into</u>:
> **expression, fit, hysterics, rage, tantrum**

Typical nouns after <u>get into</u>:
> **argument, mood**

Expressions:
> to turn into—to change into a different form
> > *The water turned into ice.*
> > *The stranger turned into a friend.*
>
> to turn something into—to change the form of something else
> > *The witch turned the prince into a frog.*
>
> to burst into flames—to suddenly be on fire
> > *The trash pile burst into flames.*

⑤ Into can indicate **interest** or **occupation.**

Pattern: *be/go* + into + noun
> *Her husband is really into football.*
> *All of her daughters went into law.*

⑥ Phrasal verbs
> break into (nonseparable)—begin an activity
> > *She was so excited that she broke into a song.*
>
> check into (nonseparable)—get information
> > *After she called the police, they went to check into the situation.*
>
> look into (nonseparable)—get information
> > *The lawyer promised to look into our case.*
>
> run into (nonseparable)—to see an acquaintance by chance
> > *We ran into each other at the mall yesterday.*
>
> talk into (separable)—to convince someone to do something
> > *She didn't want to come with us, but I talked her into it.*

① Like can mean **similar to.**

Pattern: *be, look, seem* + **like** + **noun**
She is like her sister.
They don't look like their mother.

② Like can indicate **similar behavior.**

Pattern: verb + **like** + **noun**
He talks like his father.
She swims like a duck.
Common verbs before like:
 act, behave, play, sing, talk, walk

③ Like can describe excessive behavior.

Pattern 1: verb + **noun** + **like** + **abstract noun**
She spends money like water.
Nouns commonly used with this meaning:
 anything, fun, water

Pattern 2: verb + **noun** + **like** + **adjective**
He dances like crazy.
She works like mad.

④ Like can indicate an **example.**

Pattern: noun + **like** + **noun**
They grow root vegetables, like beets, carrots, radishes, and turnips.

⑤ Like can mean **characteristic of.**

Pattern: *be* + **like** + **noun** + **to** + **verb**
It's not like you to complain.

1 **Near** means **close to** in terms of distance.
His house is near his office.
She lives near San Francisco.

2 **Near** means **within a short time.**
His birthday is near Thanksgiving.

1 **Next to** means **at the side of.**

Her best friend sits next to her at the table.
I will put my things in the basket next to yours.

1 **Of** indicates **belonging** or **connection.**

a. Of identifies a thing as a connection or **part of another thing.**
the pages of the book
the leaves of the tree

b. Of identifies people, animals, or plants as **part of a larger group.**

Pattern: noun + of + this/that + noun
the women of that family
the people of that religion
Nouns commonly used after of:
city, club, company, country, culture, descent, faith, family, gender, genus, group, ilk, organization, race, religion, society, species

c. Of identifies ideas or **works with their author,** artist, or composer.

Pattern: noun + of + noun
the works of Shakespeare
the methods of the teacher
Nouns often used before of:
essays, ideas, method, music, novels, opinion, paintings, plays, poems, poetry, songs, work, writing

d. Of identifies an individual or **special member of a group** or institution.

Pattern: noun + of + noun
the president of the class
the coordinators of the program
Nouns commonly used before of:
captain, citizen, coordinator, dictator, head, hero, heroine, leader, loser, manager, mayor, member, president, secretary, servant, star, student, teacher, treasurer, villain, winner

e. Of identifies a **person's occupation** or area of specialization.

Pattern: noun + of + noun
a professor of mathematics
students of cardiology
practitioner of medicine

f. Of indicates a **connection with a place.**

Pattern: noun + of + noun
a native of Alaska
the birds and animals of Australia
Nouns often used before of:
animal, bird, citizen, graduate, inhabitant, native, people, resident

g. Of indicates a **connection with a period of time.**
the music of the eighties
the dances of her youth
the fourth of July

the last day of the year
April of last year

2 **Of** can name another noun.

Pattern: the + noun + of + noun
They established the city of Los Angeles.
It is near the Bay of Bengal.
I don't know the name of the school.

3 **Of** can indicate the **location of a part.**

Pattern: preposition + the + noun + of + noun
The passage is in the middle of the page.
I have a knot on the back of my head.
The numbers are at the top of the page.

4 **Of** indicates a **category of description.**

Pattern: noun + of + noun
1. Typical nouns used before of indicating **category:**
   brand, category, class, color, form, kind, make, pattern, shape, size, sort, style, type
   What kind of shoes are you looking for?
   The color of your dress is beautiful.

2. Nouns used before of indicating type of **container:**
   bag, bowl, box, can, container, load, loaf, package, piece, plate, tube
   We bought two boxes of cereal.

3. Nouns used before of indicating **sensation:**
   feel, sense, smell, sound, taste, texture
   I didn't like the smell of that meat.

4. Nouns before of indicating **value:**
   cost, price, value
   The price of the dress was outrageous.

5. Nouns before of indicating **measurement:**
   depth, height, length, measurement, weight, width
   Do you know the measurement of your waist?

5 **Of** indicates a **number** or **proportion.**

Pattern 1: number/adjective + of + plural noun
   Three of the girls are our daughters.
   All of the women are from New York.
Adjectives used before of:
   all numbers
   all, another, any, both, each, either, enough, few, many, most, neither, none, plenty, several, some

Pattern 2: noun + of + plural noun
That store has a couple of books I want to buy.
A few of them are hard to find.
Nouns used before of:
a couple, a few, a lot, lots

Pattern 3: adjective + of + noncount noun
Much of the furniture is damaged.
Adjectives used before of:
all, little, much, some

Pattern 4: noun + of + noncount noun
A little of the information is correct.
A lot of it is incorrect.
Nouns used before of:
a little, a lot, lots

6 Of can **identify** abstract nouns by their source.

1. sound

Pattern: the + noun + of + noun
I heard the cry of a baby.
There was the noise of a car.
Nouns of sound commonly used before of:
buzz, crash, cry, growl, hiss, howl, hum, hush, laughter, music, noise, silence, sound, whisper

2. force

Pattern: noun + of + noun
A gust of wind blew in my face.
We all need a breath of fresh air.
Nouns of force often used before of:
breath, gush, rush, whiff

3. sight

Pattern: noun + of + noun
She had a vision of musicians playing violins.
The blue of her eyes was the color of the ocean.
Nouns of sight often used before of:
blue, color, picture, sight, vision

4. sensation

Pattern: the + noun + of + noun
The touch of his hand made me feel safe.
The smell of bread baking was wonderful.
Nouns of feeling often used before of:
feel, sense, smell, taste, texture, touch

5. expression

Pattern: noun + of + noun
He shouted words of anger.
She breathed a sigh of relief.
Nouns of expression often used before of:
cry, groan, moan, sigh, shout, smile, tears, word
Nouns of feeling often used after of:
anger, anguish, delight, elation, excitement, fear, frustration, happiness, joy, relief, sadness, surprise

7 Of can indicate **material** or **composition.**

Pattern: noun + *be* + past participle + of + noun
My new bag is made of leather.
Water is made up of hydrogen and oxygen.
Past participles used before of:
composed, formed, made, made up (used with natural phenomena)
Nouns often used after of:
aluminum, brass, cardboard, clay, copper, cotton, crystal, fabric, glass, gold, iron, jute, leather, metal, nylon, paper, plastic, platinum, polyester, rayon, sand, silk, silver, string, tin, water, wire, wood, wool

8 Of can identify **contents** or **topic.**

Pattern 1: noun + of + noun
She ate a salad of lettuce, tomatoes, and avocados.
My uncle wrote a book of short stories.
The book has pictures of flowers.
A group of students went to the museum.
Common expressions:
words of love, a sign of weakness, a method of teaching

Pattern 2: verb + of + noun
I dreamed of you.
They often talked of their youth.
Verbs commonly used before of:
complain, dream, hear, learn, sing, speak, talk, think

Pattern 3: verb + noun + of + noun
She informed me of my appointment.
Verbs used with this pattern:
advise, inform, remind, tell

Pattern 4: adjective + of + noun
She is capable of better work.
They are independent of their parents.
Adjectives commonly used with this pattern:
capable, ignorant, proud, repentant, sick, tired

Expression:
> be reminiscent of—to remind people of
> > *Your perfume is reminiscent of my mother.*

⑨ Of can indicate dedication of time to a **special purpose.**

Pattern: noun + of + noun
> *That was a day of national mourning.*
> *We stood for a moment of silence.*

Nouns often used before of:
> **day, moment, month, period, season, semester, time, week, year**

Nouns often used after of:
> **celebration, exercise, festivity, fun, happiness, meditation, mourning, prayer, quiet, reading, reflection, rest, silence, studying, thanksgiving, work**

⑩ Of can indicate **absence.**

Pattern: noun + of + noun
> *There is a need of cooperation.*
> *The lack of funds is our biggest problem.*

Nouns commonly used before of:
> **absence, dearth, necessity, need, lack, paucity, scarcity**

⑪ Of can indicate **separation.**

Pattern 1: verb + of + noun
> *He was cured of cancer.*
> *The dog died of old age.*
> *She is rid of a nuisance.*

Pattern 2: verb + noun + of + noun
> *They tried to relieve her of pain.*

Expressions:
> to get rid of—to cause to no longer have
> > *I got rid of my old car.*
>
> a change of scenery/pace—a change in place or activity
> > *We needed a change of scenery, so we went to the Caribbean.*

⑫ Of can indicate one's **feelings** toward the object.

Pattern 1: noun + of + noun
> *We appreciate the pleasure of your company.*
> *He has a love of learning.*

Nouns often used before of:
> **anguish, challenge, delight, desire, distrust, enjoyment, excitement, fear, frustration, happiness, hatred, joy, love, need, pleasure, stress**

Pattern 2: to the + noun + of + noun
We had a big party, to the delight of the children.
Nouns often used before of:
anguish, annoyance, delight, disgust, enjoyment, excitement, happiness, pleasure

⑬ **Of** can indicate an **attitude** toward something.
Pattern: *be + adjective + of + noun*
They are respectful of the environment.
Adjectives commonly used before of:
ashamed, aware, certain, conscious, disrespectful, envious, fond, inconsiderate, mindful, proud, repentant, respectful, sure, suspicious, trusting, uncertain, unsure, wary

⑭ **Of** can indicate a **reason.**
I came here because of you.
She lost all her money on account of her husband.

⑮ **Of** can describe **behavior.**

Pattern: *be + adjective + of + noun*
It was very kind of Sally to help us.
It was cruel of him to ignore her.
Adjectives commonly used with this pattern:
bad, careless, conscientious, crazy, crude, cruel, delightful, evil, good, hateful, ignorant, irresponsible, kind, mean, nice, responsible, rude, selfish, sweet, thoughtful, thoughtless, typical, unconscionable

⑯ **Of** can **describe** a noun by connecting it to a quality.

Pattern: noun + of + noun
She is a woman of honor.
They are people of integrity.
Nouns of quality often used after of:
dignity, faith, few words, good intentions, honor, integrity, high (low) morals, strength, wisdom

⑰ **Expression**
right of way—the legal right to proceed before another person
The accident was the other driver's fault because I had the right of way.

❯ Off indicates **movement** from one place to another.

Pattern 1: verb + off + noun

The car ran off the road.
We got off the train in New Orleans.

Verbs used with this pattern:

blow, come, dive, drive, fall, get, go, hop, jump, limp, move, roll, run, slide, slip, walk

Expression:

to be off (adverb)—to leave
It's late, so we must be off.

Pattern 2: verb + noun + off + noun

They shoveled the snow off the driveway.

Verbs used with this pattern:

blow, brush, clean, clear, drive, get, move, pull, push, roll, run, scrape, shove, shovel, slide, slip, sweep, take, wash

❯ Off can indicate **separation.**

Pattern: verb + off + noun

She cut off her beautiful long hair.

Verbs commonly used with this meaning:

break, chop, cut, pick, pull, saw, send, shave, take, tear, throw

❸ Off means **connected to** or **not far from.**

Pattern: *be* + off + noun

Our street is off Main Street.

Typical nouns after off:

beach, coast, highway, island, road, street, turnpike

❹ Off can indicate **behavior** that is not as usual or no longer true.

Pattern 1: *be/go* + off + ø noun

The children are off school today.
I'm glad your cousin finally went off drugs.

Nouns commonly used with this meaning:

alcohol, cigarettes, drugs, duty, school, work

Pattern 2: *be/go* + off + one's + noun

She went off her diet again.

Typical nouns:

diet, medication, medicine, pills

Expressions:

to be off course—to be going (or thinking) in the wrong direction
We got lost, and were off course for about three hours.
They got off course while doing the research, and wasted a lot of time.

to be off one's game—not be playing as well as usual
The golf champion was off his game yesterday.
to be off one's rocker—to be crazy
She feeds caviar to her cat; I think she's off her rocker.

⑤ Off can indicate **lack of contact.**

Pattern 1: verb + off + noun
Please keep off the grass.
Verbs used with this pattern:
get, keep, lay, stay

Pattern 2: verb + noun + off + noun
Please keep the dog off the grass.
Verbs commonly used with this pattern:
get, keep, move, take

⑥ Off means **cause to stop functioning.**

Pattern: verb + off + noun
Please turn off the radio.
Typical verbs with this meaning:
turn, shut, switch

⑦ Expressions

off the record—not official or public
This is off the record, but I heard that our friends got married last week.

off the charts—too high or successful to measure
Our ratings are off the charts.

off the wall—unacceptable
I'm sorry, but your ideas are really off the wall.

off-chance (noun)—unlikely possibility
I stopped by, on the off-chance that you would be at home.

off-limits (adverb)—forbidden territory
The bars are off-limits for teenagers.

off-color (adjective)—in very bad taste, with a sexual reference
I can't believe that she tells so many off-color jokes.

off-hand (adjective, adverb)—very casual, casually
He made a few off-hand remarks that I didn't appreciate.

hit it off—to become friends right away
Your sister and my brother really hit it off at the party.

be well off—to have few problems
Now that she has retired, she is pretty well off.

be better/worse off—to have fewer or more problems
She is a lot better off than she was before.

⑧ Phrasal verbs

back off (intransitive)—stop trying
The man was too aggressive and was told to back off.

beg off (intransitive)—cancel a commitment
Our babysitter didn't come; she begged off at the last minute.

break off (separable)—terminate a relationship
They couldn't agree on anything, so they broke off their engagement.

call off (separable)—cancel an event
We called the picnic off because of rain.

check off (separable)—mark on a list
She knows I was there; she checked off my name.

drop off (intransitive)—fall asleep
She kept dropping off during the meeting.

get off (nonseparable)—leave a vehicle you can walk around on
We got off the ship in Jamaica.

get off (separable)—remove, with some difficulty
She's trying to get the mud off her shoes.

goof off—waste time
Stop goofing off and get to work!

kick off (intransitive)—the beginning of an event
The conference starts tomorrow; it will probably kick off at about ten.

kill off (separable)—to destroy all members of a species
There is a danger that certain birds will be killed off.

knock off (separable)—to stop doing something
I'm sick of your teasing. Knock it off!

lay off (separable)—fire from a job
They didn't need so many workers, so they laid him off.

live off (nonseparable)—eat nothing but
We have been living off fruit and vegetables for weeks.

mark off (separable)—to designate areas for a game
They are marking the field off for the soccer match.

nod off—fall asleep
He is jet-lagged, and keeps nodding off during the day.

pull off (separable)—manage to achieve success
The clients were difficult, but he managed to pull off the sale.

put off (separable)—postpone
They put the picnic off until Tuesday.

put off (separable)—repel
They didn't invite her back; her bad manners really put them off.

round off (separable)—use the nearest whole number
Don't use all those fractions; round off all the numbers.

sell off (separable)—to sell everything
He sold off all his property and left town.

sign off (intransitive)—to end a program
  My favorite radio announcer signs off at midnight.
take off (intransitive)—leave
  The plane took off at four-thirty.
take off (separable)—remove clothing
  The sweater was too warm so he took it off.
wear off (separable)—to disappear because of wear
  I wore off the tread on my tires when I drove to California.
wipe off (separable)—to erase; to destroy completely
  The gunman wiped his fingerprints off the weapon.
write off (separable)—to no longer consider something to be of value
  He wrote off his sister when she got into trouble.

❶ On indicates location **higher than something and touching it; on top of.**

Pattern: on + noun

The newspaper is on the table.
Please sign your name on the dotted line.

❷ On indicates an **outside location.**

Pattern: on + the + noun

He was standing on the corner of First Street and Maple Avenue.
Let's have a barbecue on the balcony.

Typical nouns after on the:
balcony, beach, corner, fence, field, ground, hill, horizon, lawn, patio, porch, roof, terrace

❸ On indicates a **surface location.**

Pattern 1: on + the + noun

She rides her bicycle on the sidewalk.

Typical nouns after on the:
boardwalk, court, (baseball) diamond, field, highway, path, rink, road, rocks, screen, sidewalk, street

Pattern 2: on + ø noun

That is the only place on earth where she feels safe.

Typical nouns after on:
earth, land, page one (or any other number), solid ground, water

❹ On indicates certain **inside surface locations.**

Pattern: on + the + noun

There is a fly on the ceiling.

Typical nouns after on the:
ceiling, floor, stairs, steps, wall, window
first/second (or other number) floor

❺ On indicates surface **contact.**

Pattern: verb + noun + on + noun

The child pasted the picture on the page.

Typical verbs:
glue, hold, paste, stick

❻ On indicates **location in a part of an area.**

Pattern: be + on + the + noun + of + noun

The porch is on the side of the house.

Typical nouns after on the:
border, bottom, edge, end, exterior, inside, interior, left, outside, outskirts,
first/second (or other number) page, right, side, surface, top

7 **On** means **facing.**

Pattern: be + on + noun
Their house is on the beach.
What street is your house on?
Typical nouns:
beach, highway, river, road, street

8 **On** indicates **movement to** something; **onto.**

Pattern 1: verb + on + noun
It rained on your bicycle last night.
She jumped on the bed.
Typical verbs before <u>on</u>:
bounce, climb, fall, get, hop, jump, knock, pounce, pound, rain, stamp, step, tread

Pattern 2: verb + noun + on + noun
She poured water on the plant.
He sprinkled salt on the meat.
Typical verbs:
drip, drop, load, pour, put, shower, smear, spill, splash, spray, spread, sprinkle, squirt, throw

9 **On** indicates **travel in vehicles** in which one can walk.
She goes to work on the bus.
They went on the train to Philadelphia.
Typical nouns:
airplane, bus, ship, train
Typical verbs used before <u>on</u>:
get, go, ride, sit, travel

10 **On** indicates an **individual method of travel.**
He came over on his bike.
She was sore from riding on a horse.
Typical nouns:
all fours, bicycle, foot, one's hands and knees, motorcycle, roller blades, skate-board, skates, skis, scooter, sled, snowboard, surfboard, tiptoe, tricycle

11 **On** means **wearing.**

Pattern 1: verb + on + noun
The man has on a suit and tie.
The lady put on her new dress.

Pattern 2: verb + noun + on + noun
She put the bracelet on her wrist.
He had a hat on his head.
Typical verbs:
get, have, keep, put, try, wear

⑫ **On** indicates **physical support.**

Pattern 1: verb + on + noun
The child leaned on his father.
The children sat on small chairs.
Typical verbs used before on:
cling, hang, lean, lie, rest, sit, sleep, stand

Pattern 2: verb + noun + on + noun
She draped the cloth on the table.
He laid the sick child on the bed.
Typical verbs:
drape, hang, lay, place, put

Pattern 3: *be* + on + noun
The beads are on a string.
The popsicle is on a stick.

Expression:
to be on one's side—to support in spirit
They are my friends; I'm sure they are on my side.

⑬ **On** can indicate **trust in something or someone.**

Pattern 1: verb + on + noun
He relies on me to pay his rent.
Typical verbs used before on:
bank, bet, count, depend, rely

Pattern 2: *be* + adjective + on + noun
She is dependent on her husband.
Adjectives used before on:
based, dependent, predicated

⑭ **On** can indicate **frequency.**

Pattern: on + ø noun
He visits twice a month on average.
Nouns commonly used after on:
average, occasion, weekends, Saturdays (or other days)
nice (or other adjective) mornings, afternoons, evenings, nights

Expression:
on the whole—in its entirety
On the whole they enjoy their work.

⑮ **On** can indicate a **form of record.**

Pattern: on + ø noun
He wrote it on paper.
They recorded the song on tape.

Typical nouns:
   disk, cassette, compact disc, film, microfilm, paper, record, tape

⑯ On means **by means of.**

Pattern 1: verb + on + noun
   That car runs on diesel fuel.
   They survive on very little food.
Typical verbs used before <u>on</u>:
   live, keep alive, gain/lose weight, make do, run, scrape by, survive, train, thrive
Typical nouns used after <u>on</u>:
   calories, electricity, food, fuel, gas, income, salary

Pattern 2: verb + noun + on + noun
   I bought the furniture on credit.
   He wrote his paper on the computer.

⑰ On can mean **using** at the present time.

Pattern: *be* + on + the + noun
   The manager can't help you now; she is on the telephone.
Nouns commonly used with this pattern:
   computer, Internet, machine, telephone

Expression:
   to log on—to connect to the Internet
      Don't interrupt him now; he has just logged on.

⑱ On can indicate the **cause of a mishap.**

Pattern 1: verb + noun + on + noun
   I cut my finger on a piece of glass.
   She hurt herself on the swing.

Pattern 2: verb + on + noun
   He tripped on a fallen branch.
Verbs commonly used before <u>on</u>:
   choke, fall, stumble, trip

⑲ On can indicate a **motive for action.**

Pattern 1: verb + on + ø noun
   They went to Houston on business.
Nouns used after <u>on</u>:
   business, command, instinct, reconnaissance, request, sabbatical, spec, vacation

Expressions:
   on purpose—deliberately
      She didn't want to see him; she stayed home on purpose.
   on behalf of—in place of, for the sake of
      I went to the meeting on behalf of my mother, who was out of town.

on account of—because of
The picnic was cancelled on account of the rain.

Pattern 2: on + the + noun + of
They went overseas on the orders of the commander.
I bought the car on the recommendation of my son.
Typical nouns:
advice, assumption, authority, calculations, charge, premise, recommendation, orders

20 **On** can indicate a **type of trip.**

Pattern: verb + on + noun
The class went on an excursion around the city.
Nouns used after on:
cruise, excursion, field trip, flight, honeymoon, journey, mission, outing, safari, trip

21 **On** can indicate a **topic.**

Pattern 1: noun + on + noun
We have a good book on gardening.
He wrote a long article on the economy.
Typical nouns before on:
article, book, debate, discussion, paper, report, research, speech, thesis, thoughts

Pattern 2: verb + on + noun
She spoke on the environment.
I wish he would expound on his ideas.
Typical verbs before on:
expound, report, speak, write

22 **On** can show an **effect** of something on something else.

Pattern: noun + on + noun
We got a good buy on our car.
There is a new tax on perfume.
Typical nouns used before on:
ban, discount, embargo, encumbrance, evidence, good buy, restriction, sale, tax, war

23 **On** can indicate **possession** at the time.
She had four dollars on her.
He didn't have a gun on him.

24 **On** can indicate membership in an exclusive group.

Pattern: be + on + the + noun
She is on the basketball team and the honor roll.

Typical nouns after <u>on</u>:

board, committee, council, crew, faculty, honor roll, jury, list, payroll, squad, staff, team

㉕ On can indicate an **occasion.**

Pattern 1: on + noun
Congratulations on your graduation.
They went out to dinner on their anniversary.
Typical nouns:
anniversary, arrival, birth, birthday, death, departure, news, occasion, wedding, weekend

Pattern 2: on + ø noun
They are leaving on Saturday (or any day).

Pattern 3: on + the + noun
Example:
We are leaving on the ninth of August (or any date).
They are going to New York on the weekend.

㉖ On (adverb) can indicate **continuation.**

Pattern: verb + on
They told us to move on.
He was tired, but he drove on.
Typical verbs:
drag, drive, go, keep, live, move, press, read, run, talk, walk, work

Expression:
keep on + gerund—continue to do something
She told us to keep on reading.

㉗ On expresses **offensive action.**

Pattern 1: verb + on + noun
The troops marched on the city at dawn.
Typical expressions before <u>on</u>:
march, turn
pull a gun, pull a knife

Pattern 2: noun + on + noun
They planned a raid on the nightclub.
Typical nouns:
assault, attack, march, raid

㉘ On can indicate a **state** or condition.

Pattern 1: *be* + on + ø noun
The new windows are on order.
Our new line of products is on display at the showroom.

Typical nouns:
> **approval, board, call, course, display, duty, edge, fire, guard, high/low speed, high/low volume, hold, leave, loan, one's best behavior, order, parole, record, sale, schedule, stand-by, strike, tap, target, track, trial, vacation**

Expressions:
> on hand—available
> > *He is always on hand to help us.*
>
> on-line—connected to the Internet
> > *Every day more and more people are on-line.*
>
> on one's own—independent
> > *He is twenty-one and he lives on his own.*

Pattern 2: *be* + on + a/the + noun
> *She is on a diet.*

Typical nouns with a:
> **budget, diet, roll, spree**

Expression:
> on a roll—to be experiencing repeated success
> > *He has received four job offers; he is on a roll.*

Typical nouns with the:
> **brink, edge, line, mark, way**

Expressions:
> on the spot—to be forced to make a difficult decision
> > *The young man was on the spot when his two best friends had an argument.*
>
> on the fence—to be undecided
> > *The congressman hasn't decided which way to vote: he is on the fence.*
>
> on the air—to be broadcasting on the radio or television
> > *The news is on the air at six o'clock.*
>
> on the bench—to be the judge in court
> > *Do you know who is on the bench at her trial?*
>
> on the blink—to be broken
> > *We can't copy it; the copier is on the blink.*
>
> on the road—to be traveling
> > *Our band is going to be on the road for two weeks.*
>
> on the condition that—if
> > *You can go on the trip on the condition that you pay for it.*

29 **On** can indicate **means of communication.**
I heard it on the radio.
There are a lot of movies on television.
She found it on the Internet.

30 On can indicate the **person who pays.**
The party is on me.

Expression:

on the house—paid for by the management of the restaurant
The drinks are on the house.

31 On can mean **at the same time as.**

Pattern 1: on + verb in gerund form
She fainted on hearing the news.

Pattern 2: on + ø noun
She feeds the baby on demand.
The car is yours on receipt of the title.
Typical nouns after on:
approval, demand, receipt, reflection, second thought, sight

32 On can indicate **acquisition.**

Pattern 1: verb + on + noun
They took on five new technicians at the plant.
She wanted to add on a family room.
Typical verbs used before on:
add, bring, build, heap, load, pile, put, take

Pattern 2: verb + noun + on + noun
They forced a new assistant on us.
Typical verbs used before on:
add, build, force, heap, load, pile, put, push

Expression:

to put on—to get dressed in
She put on her shoes and went out.

33 On can indicate **attitude toward the object.**
Please have pity on the people who live there.
They agree on the important issues.

Expression:

have a crush on—to have a frivolous romantic interest in
The young boy had a crush on his teacher.

34 On can indicate **behavior** concerning the object.

Pattern 1: *be* + adjective + on + noun
The teacher is much too easy on the boys.
I think I was too rough on her yesterday.
Typical adjectives before on:
easy, hard, rough, soft, strict, tough

Pattern 2: verb + on + noun
The old lady doted on her only grandchild.
Typical verbs before on:
center, concentrate, dote, dwell, err, harp, pick, prey, put pressure, wait

Expression:
to lay hands on—to attack
If someone lays hands on you, call the police.

㉟ On can indicate a **consequence to another person.**

Pattern: verb + on + noun
We were on a family vacation and my brother got sick on us.
Please don't fall asleep on me; I need you to keep me awake.
Typical verbs:
die, cheat, faint, fall asleep, get sick, go quiet, rat, tattle, tell

㊱ Expressions

on time—at the expected time
Mary is always on time for class.

on the contrary—the opposite is true
We don't have too many books; on the contrary, we don't have enough.

on the other hand—from another viewpoint
She is never on time; on the other hand, she is a very hard worker.

on the tip of my tongue—refers to something almost remembered, but not quite
I can't remember his name, but it's right on the tip of my tongue.

on your mark—the first command of three at the start of a race
On your mark, get set, go!

to depend on—the outcome is decided by a future event
I want to have the party outside, but it depends on the weather.

㊲ Phrasal verbs

call on (nonseparable)—ask
If you need help, call on me.

carry on (intransitive)—to behave a little wildly
She carries on every night.

carry on with (nonseparable)—continue an effort
Who is going to carry on with the program when he leaves?

catch on (intransitive)—understand
My sister isn't interested in him; I'm afraid he will never catch on.

get on (nonseparable)—enter a vehicle you can walk around on; mount a horse or bicycle
We got on the bus in New York.

get on (separable)—dress with slight difficulty
See if you can get these shoes on.

get on (intransitive)—grow old
She is getting on; she is eighty-seven now.

log on (intransitive)—to connect to the Internet
She logged on to the Internet to communicate with her friend across the country.

miss out on—lose an opportunity
He missed out on a good party.

pass on (separable)—tell or give to somebody else
When you have finished reading this article, please pass it on.

pick on (nonseparable)—selectively mistreat
That teacher likes the boys but picks on the girls.

turn on (separable)—cause to function
First, you have to turn the machine on.

1 **Onto** indicates **movement** from one position to another one.

Pattern 1: **verb + onto + noun**
The child hopped onto the bed.
Typical verbs used before <u>onto</u>:
drip, fall, hop, jump, move, run, spill, step

Pattern 2: **verb + noun + onto + noun**
We moved all the books onto the desk.
Typical verbs used with this pattern:
drip, drop, move, spill, transfer

2 **Onto** indicates **knowledge of misbehavior.**

Pattern: *be* + **onto + noun.**
The police are onto that gang about the missing money.

❶ On top of indicates a position **higher than the object.**

Pattern: verb + on top of + noun

They put the blanket on top of the sheets, and the bedspread on top of the blanket.

I'm sure I left my keys on top of the desk.

❷ Expression

to be on top of something—to be sure about one's knowledge or control of something

Her son had a hard time learning math, but he is on top of it now.

1 **Opposite** means **facing; across from.**

Pattern: verb + opposite + noun

I sat opposite him at the library last night.
My house is opposite the drugstore.

46 · OUT

❶ Out can indicate **removal**.

Pattern: verb + noun + out
Please take the trash out.
Typical verbs used with <u>out</u>:
   carry, cross, cut, get, kick, leave, move, take, tear, throw

❷ Out can indicate **distribution**.

Pattern: verb + noun + out
The teacher told me to hand these papers out.
Typical verbs used with <u>out</u>:
   give, hand, mail, pass, send

❸ Out of indicates **movement from inside**.

Pattern 1: verb + out of + noun
He was freezing when he got out of the water.
Typical verbs:
   come, crawl, drink, drive, eat, fall, get, go, jump, hop, run, step

Pattern 2: verb + noun + out of + noun
She took the cake out of the oven.
Typical verbs:
   drive, get, grab, move, pour, pull, push, rip, sip, squeeze, take, tear

❹ Out of indicates **absence**.

Pattern: *be* + out of + noun
   The boss is out of the office.
   My neighbors are out of the country this month.

Expression:
   to be out of town—to be absent from one's place of residence
      The boss is out of town this week.

❺ Out of indicates a **distance from**.

Pattern: verb + out of + noun of place
   The restaurant is about three miles out of town.
   They live two blocks out of the city limits.

❻ Out of can mean **no longer in supply**.

Pattern: *be/run* + out of + plural or noncount noun
   I can't make a cake because I am out of eggs.
   They had to walk to the gas station because they ran out of gas.
Typical noncount nouns used after <u>out of</u>:
   breath, gas, luck, money, stock, time, work

7 **Out of** can mean **not as usually expected.**

Pattern: *be* + out of + noun
All her clothes are out of style.
Unfortunately, her children are out of control.
Typical nouns used after out of:
**commission, context, control, date, fashion, focus, place, practice, reach, season,
shape, style, sync, the ordinary, the way, tune**

8 **Out of** indicates the basic **ingredients** or **composition** of something.

Pattern 1: verb + noun + out of + noun
She makes the skirts out of scarves.
He crafted the tables out of twigs.

Pattern 2: past participle of verb + out of + noun
The statue was carved out of stone.
That bread is made out of whole wheat flour.
Typical verbs used before out of:
build, carve, craft, create, fabricate, fashion, make, sculpt, sew, shape

9 **Out of** can indicate a **fraction.**

Pattern 1: number + out of + number + noun
Nine out of ten people on that street have new cars.

Pattern 2: number + noun + out of + noun
Only three women out of the whole group volunteered to help.

10 **Out of** can indicate **beyond.**

Pattern: verb + out of + noun
We waved until he was out of sight.
He is out of touch with reality.
Typical nouns used after out of:
bounds, danger, hearing, line, order, sight, touch

11 **Out of** can indicate a **reason** for action.

Pattern: verb + out of + abstract noun
She invited him to the party out of kindness.
He only went out of curiosity.
Typical nouns used after out of:
**animosity, anxiety, compassion, cruelty, curiosity, fear, kindness, love, loyalty,
malice, meanness, passion, pity, respect, spite, sympathy**

12 Expressions
out of doors—outside
The children love to play out of doors.

out of it—not conscious of reality
He hasn't adjusted to his new lifestyle; he is really out of it these days.

out of the past—exactly as in the past
The music and dancing were out of the past.
She is so old-fashioned: her ideas are out of the (nineteen) sixties.

be put out—be resentful
She was really put out that you didn't invite her to your party.

⓱ Phrasal verbs

ask out (separable)—invite on a date
He asks her out all the time, but she never goes with him.

blow out (separable)—to extinguish with air
She blew out all the candles on her birthday cake.

break out (intransitive)—start suddenly
A fire broke out in the field yesterday.

check out (separable)—
1. investigate
Our air-conditioning isn't working; the repairman is coming to
check it out.
2. borrow officially
He went to the library to check out that book.

check out (of) (intransitive)—pay the bill at a hotel
Your friends checked out early this morning.
They checked out of the hotel at six o'clock.

chew out (separable)—scold
The boss really chewed her out for being late for the meeting.

chicken out (on) (nonseparable)—not act because of fear
He wanted to call the boss at home, but he chickened out.
He promised to do it, but he chickened out on me.

close out of (nonseparable)—sell all of an item, and no longer carry it
That store is closing out of small appliances, and is having a huge sale.

count out (separable)—not expect someone's participation
If you're planning a meeting for Saturday, count me out.

drop out (of) (intransitive)—leave a group or society
She didn't enjoy the club, and finally dropped out.
She dropped out of the club.

eat out (intransitive)—eat at a restaurant, rather than at home
That family eats out at least once a week.

figure out (separable)—solve; understand
She can't seem to figure out her problems.

fill out (separable)—complete in writing
Please fill out these forms.

find out (separable)—learn by investigating
Can you help me find out where they live?

get out of (nonseparable)—find an excuse to break a commitment
She said she was sick, and got out of washing the dishes.

go out with (nonseparable)—date someone
She goes out with my brother every Saturday night.

hang out (with) (intransitive)—do nothing, with friends
Those kids just hang out every day after school.
They hang out with other students.

keep out (of) (intransitive)—not enter
They told us to keep out.
They told us to keep out of their yard.

knock out (separable)—cause to lose consciousness
The champion knocked the other boxer out in the first round.

look out (for) (intransitive)—be careful
We told them to look out.
We told them to look out for cars when crossing the street.

luck out (intransitive)—be lucky
Tickets were hard to get, but we lucked out and got two in the front row.

make out (intransitive)—be successful
We sold all of our stuff at the garage sale and made out pretty well.

pass out (intransitive)—faint
She hadn't eaten all day, and she passed out.

pass out (separable)—distribute
They asked us to help pass out flyers announcing the new restaurant.

pick out (separable)—select
Here are the strawberries; pick out the best ones to serve.

point out (separable)—call attention to
The agent pointed out that the house was in a convenient neighborhood.

put out (separable)—extinguish; display
He put out the fire quickly.
She put out all her best china.

stand out (from) (intransitive)—be noticeable
The tall girl in the chorus stands out.
She stands out from all the short girls.

step out (of) (intransitive)—leave a room or building
It was so hot in there that we decided to step out for a few minutes.

talk out of (separable)—convince someone not to do something
He was going to marry that girl, but his mother talked him out of it.

try out (for) (nonseparable)—audition
She is going to try out for the musical show at school.

try out (separable)—use before buying, to find out if suitable
They let you try the car out before you buy it.

turn out (intransitive)—indicates a result
How did the dress you were making turn out?

wash out (of) (separable)—remove from clothing with soap and water
I tried to wash that spot out of my dress.

watch out (for) (intransitive)—be careful
He told her to watch out.
He told her to watch out for danger.

wear out (separable)—use until ruined
I wore my shoes out, and had to throw them away.

work out (separable)—solve a problem in a relationship
That couple had a lot of problems, but they worked them out.

work out (intransitive)—do exercise
He works out every evening.

❶ Outside (of) means **not within.**

Pattern: verb + outside (of) + noun
Don't worry, the dog is outside (of) the house.

48 · OVER

Over means **above**.

Pattern 1: verb + over + noun
The plane flew over our building.
The pictures were hanging over the sofa.
Typical verbs used before <u>over</u>:
be, bend, float, fly, hang, hover, lean, look, shine, watch

Pattern 2: verb + noun + over + noun
She hung the pictures over the sofa.
Typical verbs used with this pattern:
float, fly, hang, hold, install, nail, place, suspend

Expression:

to hold something over one's head—to control, threaten, or punish someone because of a known fact or misdeed
She knows he was fired from his last job; now she holds that over his head.

Over can mean **higher than**.

Pattern: *be* + (way) over + noun
The price of that vacation is (way) over our budget.
The water at this end of the pool is over your head.

Expression:

be over one's head—more than one can understand
I can do simple math, but that problem is way over my head.

❸ **Over** (adverb) can mean **more than**.

Pattern: over + number + noun
He was driving at over eighty miles an hour.
I have gained over five pounds this month.

❹ **Over** indicates movement **above** something and **to the other side** of it.

Pattern 1: verb + over + noun
The children jumped over the puddles on their way to school.
We had to climb over the mountain to get here.
Typical verbs used before <u>over</u>:
cross, climb, drive, get, go, hop, jump, look, run, skate, skip, step, stumble, trip

Pattern 2: verb + noun + over + noun
The young player batted the ball over the fence.
We had fun throwing rocks over the creek.
Typical verbs:
bat, carry, drive, hit, throw

❺ Over can mean **covering** something.

Pattern: **verb + noun + over + noun**
The child wore a warm jacket over her dress.
The lady sewed patches over the holes.
Typical verbs:
drape, hang, have, paint, place, pour, pull, put, sew, spread, tape, wear

❻ Over indicates **control.**

Pattern 1: *rule/preside* **+ over + noun**
She rules over her family like a tyrant.
The chairman asked me to preside over the meeting tonight.

Pattern 2: *have control/power* **+ over + noun**
They have no control over their actions.
He likes to have power over his associates.

❼ Over can mean location **on the other side of** something.
That restaurant is over the state line.
They live over the river.
Typical verbs:
be, be located, dwell, live, lie, reside

❽ All over can mean **in many parts of** a place.

Pattern: **verb + all + over + the + noun**
They have traveled all over the world.
She looked all over the city for her friend.
Typical nouns:
city, country, field, floor, house, place, playground, sidewalk, state, street, table, town, world, yard
Typical verbs:
broadcast, crawl, drive, look, roll, run, send, spill, throw, travel, walk

❾ Over can mean **during.**

Pattern 1: **over + noun**
We had an interesting discussion over breakfast this morning.
Typical nouns after over:
breakfast, coffee, dinner, drinks, lunch, snacks, tea

Pattern 2: **over + the + noun**
They decided to read the papers over the holidays.
She has been sick over the last three weeks.
Nouns commonly used with this pattern:
holidays, summer, weekend, winter
next (number) hours, days, weeks, months, years
last (number) hours, days, weeks, months, years

⑩ Over can indicate a **topic.**

Pattern: verb + over + noun
They argued over politics all night.
I wish you wouldn't fight over money.
Typical verbs used before <u>over</u>:
   argue, battle, cry, fight, grieve, gush, puzzle, sigh, worry

⑪ Over (adverb) can mean **again.**

Pattern: verb + noun + over
She didn't like my work; she told me to do it over.
Typical verbs used before <u>over</u>:
   do, read, start, write

⑫ Expressions

over the telephone—by means of telephone
   She gave me that information over the telephone.

head over heels—completely
   He is head over heels in love with her.

⑬ (All) over (adverb) means **finished.**
   The party was over at nine o'clock.

⑭ Phrasal verbs

blow over (intransitive)—be forgotten
   Don't worry about your argument with him; I'm sure it will blow over.

fall over (intransitive)—collapse
   She was sitting at her desk when she suddenly fell over.

hand over (separable)—give reluctantly
   The children had to hand over all the money they found.

have over (separable)—invite to one's home
   We want to have you over soon.

look over (separable)—review
   Please look over these papers before the meeting tomorrow.

pass over (separable)—not give an expected promotion
   She expected to be promoted to director, but she was passed over this year.

pick over (separable)—find and choose the best of a lot
   Some of these cherries are not ripe; you will have to pick them over carefully.

pull over (intransitive)—drive to the side of the road
   We were driving too fast, and the police officer made us pull over.

pull over (separable)—move to cover something
   Pull the sweater over your head.

take over (intransitive)—become the boss, or act like a boss
   The children don't like to play with that boy because he always tries to take over.

take over (separable)—carry something to another place
Please take this letter over to your neighbor.

think over (separable)—consider the pros and cons
Your offer interests us; we will think it over.

turn over (intransitive)—change position from face down, face up, or vice versa
Most babies turn over in the first six months of life.

turn over (separable)—move something from top to bottom, or vice versa
Some kids turned all the trash cans over last night.

① Past means **beyond.**

Pattern: *be* + past + noun referring to a place
  The gas station is on your left, just past the shopping center.

② Past indicates **movement in front of and beyond** a place.

Pattern: verb + past + noun
  We drove past your house on our way to the party.
  They often walk past the park.

③ Past means **older than.**

Pattern: *be* + past + noun referring to age
  His daughter is past her teens now.
  I'm sure he is past fifty.

④ Past means **no longer able** to do something.

Pattern: *be* + past + verb in gerund form
  She is bitter now, and past caring.
  The men were exhausted and past working.

⑤ Past (adverb) means **later than.**

Pattern: *be* + past + noun referring to time
  It is ten past three in the afternoon.
  They left at half past seven.

❶ Through indicates **passage within** something.

Pattern: verb + through + noun
  The children drank their milkshakes through straws.
  The highway was closed, and we had to come through the city.
Typical nouns used after <u>through</u>:
  funnel, passage, pipe, straw, tunnel
  a place—building, city, country, park, state, town

❷ Through can indicate a **gateway** or **obstacle** between two places.

Pattern 1: verb + through + noun
  We came through the front door.
  He drove through the red light and got a ticket.
Typical nouns:
  barricade, barrier, curtains, customs, door, entrance, gate, hole, intersection,
  light, slot, stop sign, window

Pattern 2: verb + noun + through + noun
  The mail carrier pushed the letters through the slot.
Typical verbs used before <u>through</u>:
  bring, carry, force, pull, push, receive, send, take

❸ Through can indicate **vision beyond something.**

Pattern: *see/show* + through + noun
  The window is so dirty that I can't see through it.
  The tablecloth needs a liner; the table legs show through it.
Typical nouns used after <u>through</u>:
  clouds, fabric, fog, glass, smoke, window

Expression:
  to see through somebody—to detect insincerity
    That woman pretends to be nice, but I can see right through her.

❹ Through can indicate the **parts beginning, between, and including.**

Pattern: from + noun + through + noun
  They have to work from Monday through Friday.
  Please read from chapter one through chapter four.

❺ Through can mean **finish something that requires effort.**

Pattern 1: verb + through + noun
  I have to get through school before I can get married.
Typical verbs used before <u>through</u>:
  get, go, live, struggle, suffer
Typical nouns after <u>through</u>:
  school, training, work

Expression:

> to go through—to experience something difficult
> *He is going through a divorce.*

Pattern 2: *be* + through + with + noun
Are you through with your exams yet?
Typical nouns used with this pattern:
course, exams, red tape, trouble

Expression:

> to go through with something—to continue doing something; to not give up
> *I can't believe you are still going to go through with your plans.*

❻ Through can indicate **in all parts of a place; throughout**

Pattern 1: verb + (all) through + the + noun
We walked all through the garden.

Pattern 2: verb + noun + (all) through + the + noun
They distributed flyers all through the neighborhood.
Typical nouns used after <u>through</u>:
building, city, country, garden, house, neighborhood, state, town

Expression:

> to go/look through something—to look at all the contents of something, hoping to find something
> *I went through my files and found these documents.*
> *I looked through my papers, but I couldn't find the certificate.*

Typical nouns used after <u>through</u>:
boxes, closets, correspondence, drawers, files, letters, notes, papers, records, things

❼ (All) through (or <u>throughout</u>) can mean **during an entire event** or period.

Pattern 1: verb + through + noun
Those women talked through the whole game.
The baby finally slept all through the night.
Typical verbs before <u>through</u>:
cheat, cry, laugh, play, sit, sleep, stay, talk, wait, watch, worry

Pattern 2: verb + noun + through + noun
She cared for her father through his illness.
Verbs commonly used with this pattern:
abuse, care for, help, ignore, wait for, wait on
Typical nouns used after <u>through</u>:
afternoon, breakfast, day, dinner, game, illness, life, lunch, meal, month, morning, night, ordeal, performance, play, time, war, wedding, week, year

Expressions:

to see something through—to stay with something until it is finished.
  Don't worry, we will see your project through.
to see somebody through—to stay with somebody until he is out of trouble.
  I will see you through this problem; I promise.

❽ Through can mean **by means of.**

Pattern: verb + noun + through + noun
We heard the news through friends.
They bought that apartment through an agency.
Typical nouns after <u>through</u>:
  agency, contacts, friends, gossip, newspaper, translator
  instruments of vision—binoculars, glasses, lenses, microscope, periscope

Expression:

to hear something through the grapevine—to get news unofficially
  We heard about your engagement through the grapevine.

❾ Through can indicate a **reason.**

Pattern: verb + noun + through + noun
She achieved success through determination and hard work.
Through an error in our accounting, we have overcharged you.
Typical nouns after <u>through</u>:
  carelessness, determination, fault, frustration, generosity, greed, hard work, help,
  kindness, luck, misinformation, negligence, selfishness
  an error, a mistake

❿ Phrasal verbs

carry/follow through (separable)—complete a project
  He has some good ideas; I hope he can carry them through.
carry/follow through with (nonseparable)—complete
  I hope he can carry through with his plans.
come through (intransitive)—perform as one has promised
  She promised to help us; I hope she comes through.
fall through (intransitive)—collapse
  All his plans to move to California fell through.
show through (separable)—to give someone a tour of a building
  When we went to Washington our congressman showed us through the Capitol.

① **Throughout** means **in all parts** of a place.
There are spiders throughout the building.

② **Throughout** means during **an entire period of time.**
She stays at the beach throughout the summer.

1 To indicates the **destination of a verb.**

Pattern 1: verb + to + ø noun
I'm going to bed.
They ride to school on the bus.
Nouns commonly used after to:
bed, breakfast, church, dinner, jail, lunch, school, work

Exception:
go ø home
It is time to go home.
They went home on the bus.

Pattern 2: verb + to + the + noun
We go to the park every afternoon.
Call when you get to the office.
Verbs often used with to:
come, drive, extend, fall, fly, get, go, hike, move, return, ride, rise, run, send, ship, sink, walk

Expression:
to rise to the occasion—to force oneself to act correctly
I was surprised when he walked in, but I rose to the occasion and shook his hand.

2 To indicates the **destination of a noun.**

Pattern 1: noun + to + noun
The train to New York leaves at six o'clock.
We wanted to go on a cruise to the Caribbean.
Typical nouns used before to:
airplane, bridge, bus, climb, cruise, flight, highway, path, race, road, subway, train, trip, way

Pattern 2: noun + *be* + to + noun
The train is to New York.
His question is to me.
Typical nouns used before to:
answer, card, donation, explanation, gift, letter, memo, offer, petition, present, proposal, question, request, suggestion

3 To indicates a **transfer** from a person or place.

Pattern: verb + noun + to + noun
He delivers the mail to the office.
She mentioned her plans to me.
Typical verbs used before to:
bring, carry, deliver, describe, distribute, donate, explain, give, hand, introduce, lend, mention, pass, present, read, recommend, reveal, send, shout, show, sing, speak, submit, suggest, take, tell, write

④ To indicates a **beneficiary.**

Pattern 1: verb + noun + to + noun
They made a toast to the bride and groom.

Typical verbs used with this pattern:
award, dedicate, devote, give, make

Typical nouns used before to:
award, dedication, gift, memorial, monument, present, plaque, remark, scholarship, statement, toast

Expression:
as a favor to—for the benefit of
We came to help you as a favor to your father.

Pattern 2: to + one's + noun
If you shout, someone will come to your aid.
It is to your benefit to join the credit union.
The police came to my rescue when my car broke down.

⑤ To indicates an **effect on the recipient.**

Pattern 1: *be* + noun + to + noun
He is a credit to his mother and father.
The airplane noise is a disturbance to the neighborhood.

Nouns commonly used before to:
annoyance, bother, challenge, credit, detriment, discredit, disturbance, help, nuisance

Pattern 2: *be* + adjective + to + noun
His calls are very annoying to me.

Typical adjectives used before to:
abhorrent, acceptable, annoying, beneficial, boring, confusing, crucial, distasteful, detrimental, disturbing, fascinating, gratifying, harmful, helpful, hurtful, important, meaningful, obnoxious, pleasing, precious, preferable, repulsive, satisfying, unacceptable, unfavorable, unimportant, vexing, worrisome

Expression:
to be to one's taste—to be personally pleasing to someone
The apartment is large and expensive, but it's not to my taste.

Pattern 3: to + one's + noun
To my surprise, everybody was at work on Saturday.
To their delight, the campaign was a great success.

Typical nouns:
astonishment, chagrin, delight, disappointment, discomfort, disgrace, disgust, embarrassment, horror, satisfaction, surprise

⑥ To can indicate a **reaction.**

Pattern 1: verb + to + noun
She responded to my letter right away.
I hope you don't object to my offer of help.

Typical verbs used before to:

adapt, admit, agree, appeal, consent, listen, object, pay attention, prefer, react, relate, reply, respond, revert, subscribe

Pattern 2: noun + to + noun
She has an allergy to that medicine.
Do you have an answer to that question?

Typical nouns:

allergy, answer, appeal, aversion, consent, objection, preference, reaction, relation, reply, response

Pattern 3: *be* + adjective + to + noun
She is allergic to that medicine.
We are indebted to you for helping us.

Typical adjectives:

accustomed, allergic, grateful, indebted, thankful

7 **To** can indicate someone's **behavior toward another person.**

Pattern: *be* + adjective + to + noun
He was very cruel to me.
She has been hostile to her neighbors.

Typical adjectives:

affectionate, appreciative, attentive, available, charming, cold, considerate, cordial, cruel, devoted, dreadful, faithful, friendly, gracious, hospitable, hostile, inconsiderate, kind, loyal, mean, nice, obedient, open, pleasant, polite, respectful, sassy, warm

8 **To** can indicate **attachment.**

Pattern 1: verb + noun + to + noun
We will paste the wallpaper to the bedroom walls.
She pinned the flowers to my lapel.

Pattern 2: *be* + past participle of verb + to + noun
Your paper is stapled to mine.
The gum is stuck to my shoe.

Typical verbs used with these patterns:

add, affix, adhere, apply, attach, glue, hold, paste, pin, press, nail, screw, sew, staple, stick, tape

9 **To** indicates the **end of a period of time; until.**

Pattern: from + to + noun
They work from morning to night.
He was here from two to five.

10 **To** means **before,** in telling time.

Pattern: It + *be* + number of minutes + to + hour
It is ten (minutes) to three in the afternoon.
It was a quarter (fifteen minutes) to four.

⑪ To can indicate **continuous repetition of an action.**

Pattern 1: verb + from + noun + to + same noun
We went from door to door with our information sheets.
The bus rocked from side to side.
Common expressions:
door to door, house to house, place to place, side to side

Pattern 2: noun + hyphen + same noun + noun
They have door-to-door service.

⑫ To can indicate a **comparison of value.**

Pattern 1: *be* **+ adjective + to + noun**
His work is comparable to hers.
Your car is similar to mine.
Typical adjectives:
comparable, inferior, preferable, similar, superior

Pattern 2: *compare* **+ noun + to + noun**
Please don't compare my work to yours.

Pattern 3: *compared* **+ to + noun**
She is of medium height, but compared to her sister, she is tall.

⑬ To can indicate a **problem** or **solution.**

Pattern: noun + to + noun
The strike is a threat to our survival.
She knows the secret to success.
Typical nouns used before to:
Problems: **barrier, obstacle, threat**
Solutions: **answer, antidote, boost, clue, directions, guide, instructions, key, secret, solution**

⑭ To can indicate **ownership, membership,** and **connection.**

Pattern 1: *belong/pertain* **+ to + noun**
The book belongs to me.
Her friends belong to that club.
This discussion does not pertain to you.

Pattern 2: adjective + to + noun
Your comments are not pertinent to this topic.
Adjectives used with this meaning:
attached, attributable, committed, connected, dedicated, engaged, exclusive, important, married, obligated, pertinent, promised, relevant, related, seconded, tied

⑮ To can indicate an **exclusive relationship.**

Pattern: the + noun + to + noun
This is the key to my front door.
Have you seen the jacket to my new suit?
She is the new secretary to the chairman.
Typical nouns:
assistant, case, cover, door, jacket, key, knob, lid, part, secretary, strap, ticket, top

⑯ To indicates the **accompaniment of sound.**

Pattern: verb + to + noun
We danced to the rhythm of the music.
I wake up to the noise of the city.
Typical nouns:
beat, blare, buzz, honk, hum, music, noise, rhythm, roar, sound, strum, tune

⑰ To means **leading to an extreme condition.**

Pattern: verb + noun + to + noun
He tore the paper to pieces.
She drives him to distraction.
Common expressions:
beat/grind to a pulp
bore to death
carry to extremes
chill to the bone
cook to perfection
drive to distraction/insanity
grind to dust
move to tears
push/carry/take to the limits
sing/rock to sleep
smash to bits
soak to the skin
starve/freeze to death
tear to pieces/shreds

⑱ To indicates an **upper limitation** of an approximation.

Pattern: number + to + number
It is two to two-and-a-half feet long.
He is thirty-eight to forty years old.

⑲ To indicates a **relationship** between the subject and the object.

Pattern 1: noun + *be* + adverb + to + noun, to show location
The library is close to the park.
The new theater is adjacent to the mall.

Typical adverbs:
at an angle, close, next

Pattern 2: noun + *be* + adjective + noun
That line is parallel to this one.
Typical adjectives:
adjacent, parallel, perpendicular

Pattern 3: noun + to + noun, to indicate position
They sat back to back.
She came face to face with danger.

Pattern 4: number + to + number, to give the score of a game
The score was three to two.

Pattern 5: amount + to + amount, to show equality
There are four quarts to a gallon.

Pattern 6: amount + to + amount, to show ratio
He gets thirty miles to a gallon on the highway in his new car.

⑳ To can indicate **restriction.**

Pattern 1: verb + noun + to + noun
We limited him to three meals a day, with no snacks.
They confined her to jail for thirty-six hours.
Typical verbs:
bind, confine, hold, limit, restrict, sentence, tie

Pattern 2: past participle of verb (adjective) + to + noun
He is limited to three meals a day.
She is confined to jail for thirty-six hours.

㉑ Expressions

to subscribe to—to pay for and receive a periodical regularly
How many magazines do you subscribe to?
She subscribes to three daily newspapers.

from time to time—occasionally
He calls me from time to time.

to be used to/to be accustomed to + noun—to have adapted
He is dizzy because he is not used to the altitude.
She is nervous because she is not used to driving in traffic.

㉒ Phrasal verbs

come to (intransitive)—regain consciousness
She fainted a few minutes ago, but fortunately came to right away.

see to (nonseparable)—take responsibility for a future action
You don't have to make reservations; we will see to that.

look forward to (nonseparable)—await with pleasure
We are looking forward to seeing you soon.

1 **Toward** means **in the direction of a place.**

Pattern 1: verb + toward + noun
She ran toward the playground to see her friends.
Let's head toward the park.
Typical verbs:
blow, fly, go, head, hike, look, march, move, point, run, sail, turn, walk

Pattern 2: verb + noun + toward + noun
He guided us toward the cave.
They directed the girls toward the path.
Typical verbs:
direct, guide, lead, push, pull, shove, throw

2 **Toward** indicates **attitude** about something.

Pattern 1: *be* **+ adjective + toward + noun**
She is very affectionate toward her parents.
They have been cool toward his proposals.
Typical adjectives:
affectionate, charitable, considerate, cool, friendly, gracious, hospitable, inhospitable, menacing, spiteful, warm

Pattern 2: noun + toward + noun
His feelings toward her have not changed.
Typical nouns before toward:
attitude, behavior, conduct, demeanor, feelings

3 **Toward** indicates the **direction of action.**

Pattern: verb + toward + noun
They are heading toward an agreement.
We worked toward a happy conclusion for everyone.
Typical nouns after toward:
agreement, argument, conclusion, ending, goal, vote
Typical verbs:
head, lean, push, take steps, work

4 **Toward** indicates the object of a **contribution** or **partial payment.**

Pattern: verb + toward + noun
The money will go toward helping the family.
She contributes toward his monthly expenses.
Typical verbs:
contribute, donate, give, go, help

❶ Towards means **near a period of time.**

Pattern 1: towards + noun

I always feel hungry towards dinnertime.

Typical nouns used after <u>towards</u>:

dawn, dinnertime, dusk, evening, lunchtime, mid-afternoon, midnight, noon

Pattern 2: towards + the + end/middle + of + the + noun

We start getting ready for school towards the end of the summer.

Typical nouns used with this pattern:

class, concert, course, day, fall, flight, game, month, party, period, season, semester, show, spring, summer, trip, vacation, week, winter, year

❶ Under means **in a lower position** than something else.

Pattern 1: verb + under + noun
We sat under the tree and had a picnic.

Pattern 2: verb + noun + under + noun
Let's put the desk under the window; then we'll have a great view.

❷ Under means **covered by something else; underneath.**

Pattern 1: verb + under + noun
The children hid under the table, thinking we couldn't see them.
Typical verbs before <u>under</u>:
be, hide, lie, rest, sit, sleep, stand, wait, walk

Pattern 2: verb + noun + under + noun
She stores all her boxes under the bed.
Typical verbs:
bury, find, hide, place, push, put, store, wear

❸ Under means **less than.**

Pattern: under + noun
I'm sure she was driving under the speed limit.
He has three children under age ten.
Nouns commonly used after <u>under</u>:
any number, age, average, height, limit, maximum, minimum, norm weight

Expression:
to be under age—to not be old enough to do something
She can't vote because she is under age.

❹ Under can indicate **control.**

Pattern 1: under + noun
Under this boss we have little freedom to express our own ideas.
You have a lot more benefits under the new insurance policy.
Typical nouns used after <u>under</u>:
boss, coach, contract, dictator, doctor, general, king, mayor, policy, principal, president, professor, supervisor, teacher

Pattern 2: under + the + noun + of + noun
She is under the care of a doctor.
Typical nouns after <u>under the</u>:
administration, care, control, dictatorship, direction, eye, management, presidency

Pattern 3: under + ø + noun
The children are under supervision at all times.
They were arrested under orders of the chief.

Typical nouns:
control, orders, supervision, surveillance

⑤ Under can indicate a **current situation or state:**

Pattern 1: *be* + **under** + ø **noun**
Those two thugs are under investigation by the police.
That problem is still under discussion by the board.
Typical nouns used after <u>under</u>:
consideration, construction, discussion, investigation, suspicion

Pattern 2: *be* + **under** + **noun**
They are under the influence of their new friends.
Typical nouns used after <u>under</u>:
circumstances, conditions, impression, influence

⑥ Under can identify the **category of a noun** in written reference material.

Pattern: *look up/find* + **noun** + **under** + **name of category**
You can find my name under "Y" in the telephone book.
I looked up butterflies under "Insects" in my encyclopedia.

1 **Underneath** means **in a lower position** than something else.
The sheets are underneath the blankets on the shelf.

2 **Underneath** means **covered by.**
I found my jacket underneath the other coats.

3 **Underneath** indicates **concealed feelings.**
Underneath her smile there is a lot of heartache.
He is really very kind underneath his stern appearance.

57 · UNTIL

1 **Until** indicates the **time of change** of an activity or situation.

Pattern 1: verb + until + time
They waited until six o'clock.
The boys studied until midnight.

Pattern 2: verb + until + beginning of event
They lived here until their wedding; then they left.
She was busy until her graduation.
They didn't watch the game until halftime.

❶ Up indicates **movement to a higher place.**

Pattern 1: verb + up + noun
The cat climbed up the tree.
She always walks up the steps to the fifth floor.
Typical verbs used before <u>up</u>:
climb, creep, go, jump, move, pop, race, run, walk

Pattern 2: verb + noun + up + noun
Bring the box up the steps.
Typical verbs used with this pattern:
bring, carry, drag, heave, move, send, take

❷ Up (adverb) indicates **location at a high place.**

Pattern: *be* **+ up**
The balloon is up.

Expression:
to be up—to be awake
I am up every day by eight o'clock.

❸ Up indicates **location further along** the way.

Pattern: verb + up + noun
Their farm is three miles up the road.
She lives two blocks up the street.

❹ Up indicates **movement along a way.**

Pattern 1: verb + up + noun
She is going to travel up Route 66.
Nouns commonly used after <u>up</u>:
highway, path, road, street, turnpike, way

Pattern 2: verb + noun + up + noun
We will drive four more miles up the highway.

❺ Up indicates movement **against a current of water.**

Pattern: verb + up + noun
They swam up the river for exercise.
Typical verbs used before <u>up</u>:
cruise, drive, go, row, sail, swim

❻ Up indicates a **desired result.**

Pattern: verb + up + noun
They are trying to drum up support.
Typical verbs:
drum, round, scrape, work

Expression:

to get up (enough) energy—to try to force oneself to act
She was exhausted, but she got up enough energy to cook dinner for her family.

7 **Up** indicates **creativity.**

Pattern: verb + up + noun
We dreamed up a wonderful idea.
Typical verbs used before up:
draw, dream, make, think

8 **Up** can indicate **division into pieces.**

Pattern: verb + up + noun
She chopped up the onions and peppers.
They divided up all the money.
Typical verbs:
break, blow, chop, cut, divide, tear

9 **Expressions**

up and down the room—constant movement from one side of the room to the other
He was so nervous that he walked up and down the room all night.

to count up to—to count as far as a number
The baby can count up to ten already.

to be up to date—to have current knowledge or records
The president is up to date on all the important issues.
It's important to keep the files up to date.

to make up one's mind—to decide
Make up your mind between the red dress and the black one.

to be up to someone—to be the responsibility of someone to decide
I don't care what movie we see; it's up to you.

to be up in arms (about)—to be angry
The employees are up in arms over the decrease in benefits.

to be up to one's ears—to the extreme
Her brother is up to his ears in work.

to be up a creek—to be in a difficult situation
My partner left with all my money and now I'm up a creek.

10 **Phrasal verbs**

act up (intransitive)—misbehave
The children always act up just before the school holidays begin.

add up (intransitive)—make sense
She claims to have lots of friends, yet she is always alone; it doesn't add up.

back up (intransitive)—reverse
The hardest part about driving a car is backing up.

blow up (intransitive)—get angry
   The girl's father blew up when she got home so late.

blow up (separable)—make bigger
   These photographs are too small; we should blow them up.

bone up on (nonseparable)—do an intensive study or review of
   He wanted to bone up on European history before he went on the tour.

boot up (separable)—start a computer
   We shut the computer down and then booted it up again.

break up (with) (intransitive)—end a relationship
   It's always sad when a family breaks up.
   The girl cried when she broke up with her boyfriend.

break up (separable)—end
   The neighbors didn't like our noisy party and told us to break it up.

bring up (separable)—raise
   She brought the children up by herself.

bring up (separable)—mention a new topic
   At the meeting, the lady brought up the parking problem in our neighborhood.

brush up (on) (nonseparable)—practice to relearn old skills
   He wants to brush up on his Spanish before he goes to Mexico.

burn up (separable)—be destroyed by fire (something small)
   All of her papers and books burned up in the fire.

burn up (separable)—make angry
   Those silly gossips really burn me up.

call up (separable)—contact someone by telephone
   He comes home from school and calls all his friends up.

catch up (with) (intransitive)—reach the place or level of another person or people
   He has been sick and needs some time to catch up.
   It will be hard for him to catch up with the other students.

catch up on (nonseparable)—get back to a normal situation
   After staying up late every night, I need to catch up on sleep.

cheer up (intransitive)—be happier
   She needs to cheer up.

cheer up (separable)—make someone happier
   She needs someone to cheer her up.

clean up (intransitive)—clean thoroughly
   They promised to clean up after the party.

clean up (separable)—clean thoroughly
   They promised to clean the house up after the party.

close up (intransitive)—close for business
   The shops close up in the afternoon, and re-open in the evening.

close up (separable)—stop operating a business
   They closed the shop up last year.

come up to—approach
   They came up to us and asked for help.

cover up (separable)—hide the facts
They committed a crime and then covered it up.

dress up—put on more formal clothes than usual
She always dresses up for parties.

face up to (nonseparable)—confront
She had to stop dreaming and face up to the truth.

feel up to (nonseparable)—feel good enough for an activity
He is a lot better, but he still doesn't feel up to going to work.

fill up (separable)—put in all that the container will hold
If you use my car, please fill it up with gas.

get up (intransitive)—rise
She gets up at six o'clock every morning.

get up (separable)—lift or remove something with some difficulty
Will you help me get these boxes up the steps?

give up (intransitive)—surrender
We won the game because the other team gave up and went home.

give up (on) (intransitive)—stop trying
She tried to convince her daughter to go back to school, but she finally gave up.
She finally gave up on her daughter.

give up (separable)—stop using something
He tried to stop smoking cigarettes, but found it hard to give them up.

grow up (intransitive)—become an adult
Her son wants to be a doctor when he grows up.

hang up (intransitive)—put the phone down to end a telephone call
You have dialed the wrong number; hang up and try again.

hang up (separable)—put clothing on a hook or hanger
After you wash this dress, you should hang it up.

hang up on (nonseparable)—rudely end a telephone call during a conversation
When she refused his invitation, he got angry and hung up on her.

hold up (intransitive)—continue in good condition
The bike is in good shape now, but I don't know how long it will hold up.

hold up (separable)—delay
The traffic on the bridge held us up for two hours.

hurry up (intransitive)—go faster
Please hurry up! We're late.

keep up (intransitive)—stay at the level of the others
The other hikers walked faster, and we couldn't keep up.

keep up (separable)—continue
You are doing a great job. Keep it up!

keep up with (nonseparable)—go as fast as
Please don't walk so fast; I can't keep up with you.

line up (intransitive)—form a line for service in order
We always line up to buy tickets.

line up (separable)—make an arrangement with someone
   We lined up a great band for our dance.
look up (separable)—search in a guide or directory
   If you want her phone number, look it up in the telephone directory.
look up to (nonseparable)—respect
   Everybody in the department looks up to the director; she is wonderful.
make up (with) (intransitive)—become friends again after an argument
   They had a big fight, but they made up last night.
   They made up with each other at the party.
make up (separable)—do missed work at a later time
   She missed the test, but the teacher said she could make it up next week.
make up to (separable)—do a favor to pay for a damage
   She hurt his feelings, then made it up to him by inviting him to her party.
mark up (separable)—increase the price
   Those shoes were cheaper last year; they have marked them up.
mix up (with) (separable)—put with other things
   She put the ingredients in a bowl and mixed them all up.
   They mixed the eggs up with the butter and sugar.
mix up (separable)—confuse
   The sisters look so much alike; I mix them up all the time.
pass up (separable)—miss an opportunity
   She had a chance to continue her studies, but she passed it up to get married.
pick up (intransitive)—increase in momentum or pace
   Business is very slow this season; we hope it will pick up soon.
pick up (separable)—lift
   When I dropped my bracelet on the sidewalk, he picked it up and handed it to me.
run up (separable)—increase charges through excessive use
   He made a lot of long-distance calls and ran up my phone bill.
set up (separable)—arrange
   We set the appointment up for November.
set up (separable)—cause an innocent person to be blamed for something
   He is not guilty of the theft; the hoodlums set him up.
set up (separable)—establish in a career or business
   His uncle set him up in the family trade.
show up (intransitive)—appear
   We will leave early if everyone shows up on time.
show up (separable)—appear to be better than someone else
   They practiced the dance steps at home and showed everybody else up at the party.
sign up—register
   We are signing up for your course.
sign up (separable)—arrange an activity for someone
   They signed us up to work on Thursday night.

slip up (intransitive)—make a mistake
We intended to send the package last week, but our workers slipped up.

stand up (intransitive)—move to one's feet; be on one's feet
When the president entered the room, everyone stood up.
When you teach school, you have to stand up all day.

stand up (separable)—miss a commitment without explaining
He went to pick her up but she wasn't there; she had stood him up.

step up (separable)—increase the speed
Step it up a little; we need to go faster.

take up (separable)—pursue a new interest
She took up knitting when she was pregnant.

take up (separable)—to shorten
The pants are too long; we will have to take them up.

tear up (separable)—rip into small pieces
The letter made her so angry that she tore it up.

throw up (intransitive)—vomit
The poor child got sick and threw up.

turn up (intransitive)—appear
She is very unreliable; we never know if she will turn up.

turn up (separable)—increase in volume or speed
Turn the radio up; this is a great song.

wake up (intransitive)—open one's eyes after sleeping
What time do you usually wake up?

wake up (separable)—cause someone to stop sleeping
Please wake me up in the morning.

wrap up (separable)—finish a session
We've been practicing for three hours; let's wrap it up.

write up (separable)—explain in writing
His ideas were good, and they asked him to write them up.

❶ With means **in the company of.**

Pattern 1: verb + with + noun
She is with her sister.
I danced with him.
Typical verbs used before <u>with</u>:
be, chat, converse, dance, drink, eat, go, leave, live, play, stay, study, talk, travel, walk, work

Pattern 2: verb + noun + with + noun
She spent the weekend with us.
Typical verbs used with this pattern:
dance, drink, eat, leave, play, spend, study

Expressions:

to be tied up with—to be occupied with at the moment
He can't come to the phone; he is tied up with a client.

to be in a discussion with—to be talking seriously to
The boss is in a discussion with the manager right now.

❷ With means **in the same place as.**

Pattern 1: *be* + with + noun
My hat is with my scarf.

Pattern 2: verb + noun + with + noun
Put your coat with mine.
She left her children with the babysitter.
Typical verbs:
keep, leave, put, store

❸ With can mean **added together.**

Pattern: noun + with + noun
She always drinks her coffee with sugar.
The hotel with meals will cost 200 dollars a day.

❹ With can describe something by indicating what it **has.**

Pattern 1: noun + with + noun
Did you see a woman with a baby a few minutes ago?
I have an article with pictures for my presentation.

Pattern 2: *be* + past participle + with + noun
You will be provided with two sets of keys.
Past participles used with this pattern:
caught, discovered, found, furnished, provided, seen

Expression:

> to be blessed with—to be lucky to have
>> *He is blessed with good health and good looks.*

5 **With** can describe a **manner of behavior.**

Pattern 1: verb + with + noun

> *Please handle the piano with care.*
> *They accepted the proposal with enthusiasm.*

Typical nouns used after <u>with</u>:

anger, care, compassion, courage, delight, discretion, disdain, distress, enthusiasm, fear, feeling, glee, grace, gratitude, happiness, hatred, humility, indifference, kindness, joy, love, optimism, pleasure, pride, regard, sadness, shame, skill, sympathy, tenderness, thanks, understanding

Pattern 2: verb + noun + with + noun

> *She greeted us with a big smile.*
> *He always starts work with a grumble.*

Typical nouns used after <u>with</u>:

air, cry, expression, frown, greeting, grumble, grunt, handshake, hug, kiss, look, promise, question, shudder, sigh, smile, smirk, thank you, word

Pattern 3: *be* + adjective + with + noun (thing)

> *Please be careful with the piano.*
> *I hope he is successful with the mission.*

Typical adjectives:

awkward, careful, clumsy, creative, dexterous, quick, skillful, slow, successful, talented, unsuccessful

Pattern 4: *be* + adjective + with + noun (person)

> *She is very patient with me.*
> *He hasn't been sympathetic with her problems.*

Typical adjectives:

awkward, belligerent, curt, flexible, forthcoming, frank, friendly, generous, helpful, honest, impatient, open, patient, stiff, sympathetic, truthful

6 **With** can describe someone's **feelings about something.**

Pattern: *be* + adjective + with + noun

> *The child was bored with her toys.*
> *They are very happy with their new home.*

Typical adjectives used with this pattern:

bored, comfortable, content, delighted, disappointed, frustrated, happy, impressed, pleased, satisfied, thrilled, uncomfortable, unhappy, upset

Expression:

> to be in love with—to have a romantic feeling toward
>> *He is (madly) in love with her.*

❼ With can indicate **a working relationship.**

Pattern 1: *be* + with + noun
She is with a real estate company.

Pattern 2: *be* + past participle + with + noun
He is involved with that organization.
They are not concerned with our group.

Pattern 3: *work* + with + noun
His mother works with us.

❽ With can indicate the **instrument or tool used** for an action.

Pattern 1: verb + with + noun
She writes with a pen.
Typical verbs used before with:
color, clean, cut, dig, draw, eat, paint, serve, sweep, wash, write

Pattern 2: verb + noun + with + noun
The boy drew a flower with his crayons.
I swept the garage with a big broom.
Typical verbs:
attach, clean, clear, cut, dig, draw, dry, eat, erase, fasten, hit, move, nail, open, paint, plow, season, serve, sweep, wash, write

❾ With can indicate a noun that **covers or fills an area.**

Pattern: verb + noun + with + noun
She filled the pitcher with lemonade.
They planted the bed with white flowers.
Typical verbs:
cover, cram, fill, frost, heap, ice, pack, paint, plant, smear, spread, sprinkle, stuff

❿ With can indicate **struggle**

Pattern 1: verb + with + noun
My colleague disagrees with the management.
He is always fighting with his brother.
Typical verbs:
argue, clash, compete, conflict, differ, disagree, fight, quarrel, wrestle

Expression:

to have it out with—to express anger verbally
After two years of frustration, he finally had it out with his boss.

Pattern 2: *have* + a + noun + with
She has an argument with him every morning.
They are having a quarrel with the neighbors right now.
Typical nouns:
argument, bout, contest, disagreement, fight, match, quarrel

Pattern 3: *be + in + noun + with*
> *She is in competition with him for the promotion.*
> *It's too bad your ideas are in conflict with those of the majority.*

⑪ With can indicate **support or cooperation.**

Pattern 1: verb + with + noun
> *They are cooperating with the authorities.*
> *You have to comply with the rules.*

Typical verbs:
> **agree, collaborate, comply, concur, cooperate, empathize, harmonize, help, negotiate, sympathize, work**

Expressions:
> to get along with—to cooperate with
> > *I get along with my roommate, even though she is not my best friend.*
> to be with—to support
> > *Don't be nervous when you are giving your speech; we are all with you.*

Pattern 2: verb + a + noun + with + noun
> *She signed a contract with us.*

Typical nouns:
> **agreement, business, contract, friendship, partnership, relationship**

Expression:
> to do business with—to have negotiations with
> > *We don't do business with them anymore.*

Pattern 3: *be + in + noun + with + noun*
> *Are you in agreement with the decisions they made?*

Typical nouns before <u>with</u>:
> **accord, agreement, cahoots, concert, collaboration, compliance, concurrence, cooperation, harmony, partnership, sympathy**

⑫ With means **at the same time as.**
> *He rises with the sun.*
> *They opened the show with a song.*

Typical verbs:
> **begin, celebrate, close, dedicate, end, start**

⑬ With means **at the same rate as.**
> *Wine improves with age.*
> *Wisdom comes with experience.*
> *With time, you will forget.*

⑭ With means **in the same direction as.**

Pattern: verb + with + the + noun
> *It will take longer because we will be with the traffic.*
> *They drifted down the river with the current.*

Typical verbs used before with:
be, cruise, drift, drive, float, go, ride, sail
Typical nouns used after with the:
current, flow, tide, traffic, wind

⑮ With can indicate **separation.**

Pattern: verb expression + with + noun
I hate to part with my old books.
Our company severed relations with that client years ago.
He is through with her; he doesn't want to see her again.
Typical verb expressions used before with:
be finished, be through, break up, cut ties, fall out, part, part company, sever relations, split up

⑯ With is used in a **comparison** or **contrast.**

Pattern 1: noun + verb + with + noun
Your blouse clashes with your skirt.
Verbs commonly used with this pattern:
clash, compare, contrast, go, look good

Pattern 2: compare/contrast + noun + with + noun
Let's compare this computer with that one.

⑰ With can indicate **equality.**

Pattern: *be* **+ adjective + with + noun**
This side is not even with that side.
Our team is tied with theirs: the score is two to two.
Typical adjectives used before with:
comparable, even, level, on a par, parallel, tied

⑱ With can indicate the **cause of a condition.**

Pattern 1: adjective + with + noun
The branches of the trees were heavy with snow.
The girl's face is wet with tears.

Pattern 2: verb in gerund form + with + noun
The newlyweds were beaming with happiness.
Typical verbs used before with:
aching, beaming, crying, dancing, fuming, screaming, shouting, smiling, trembling
Typical nouns used after with:
anger, fear, glee, happiness, joy, mirth, rage, shame, zeal

Pattern 3: with + the + noun
With the traffic in this city, it takes a long time to get to work.
Their lifestyle changed completely with the birth of their first baby.

Typical nouns used after <u>with the</u>:
   arrival, bills, birth, change, crime, death, decrease, departure, guests, increase, move, problems, rain, traffic, trouble, worries

   Pattern 4: with + (all) + possessive noun or pronoun + noun
   With all his talent, he should be famous.
   She is quite popular, with all her beauty and charm.
   Typical nouns after <u>with</u>:
   beauty, charm, education, influence, intelligence, money, power, talent

⑲ With can mean **despite.**

   Pattern: with + (all) + possessive noun or pronoun + noun
   I love him with all his faults.
   With all her problems, she is quite serene.

⑳ Expressions

   to be with someone—to follow or understand
   Please repeat that; I'm not with you.

   to be charged with something—to be formally accused of a crime
   The boy was charged with breaking and entering.

   Down with something—a rallying call to eliminate oppressors
   Down with the tyrants!

   Off with someone—a call for someone to leave
   Off with you, and don't come back!

㉑ Phrasal verbs

   (get) on with (nonseparable)—to start something right away
   Let's get on with this job; I want to go home early.
   On with the show!

   get away with—escape a misdeed without penalty
   He tore up his parking fine and got away with it.

   put up with—tolerate
   The house is beautiful, but I can't put up with the noise of the airplanes.

1 **Within** means **not outside a place.**

Pattern: *be* + within + noun
Those schools are within the county jurisdiction.
There is too much commotion within the building.
Typical nouns used after within:
area, building, city, country, county, jurisdiction, state, territory, walls

2 **Within** means **less than a period of time.**
I will return within the hour.
He will finish within five minutes.

3 **Within** means **less than a distance.**
There is a hospital within five miles of the school.
The storm was within ten miles of our town.

4 **Within** means **possible; not exceeding the limits of something.**

Pattern: *be* + within + (one's) noun
At last, the beach is within sight!
A fortune is within our reach if we are lucky.
Typical nouns after within:
bounds, hearing, range, sight, reach, the law, the limit, the rules

5 **Expression**

to keep within the family—to not reveal something to anyone who is not a
family member
That man has a strange history, but they keep it within the family.

❶ Without indicates the **absence of somebody.**
I can't live without you.
Please don't leave without me.

❷ Without means **not having.**

Pattern: verb + without + (any) noun
That young mother manages without any help.
We are without money this month.

❸ Without means **not using.**

Pattern: verb + noun + without + noun
We did the crossword puzzle without a dictionary.
She can't read without her glasses.

❹ Without means **not performing an action.**

Pattern: without + verb in gerund form
She passed the test without studying.
He left without saying good-bye.

❺ Expressions

without a doubt—certainly
She is without a doubt the best chairman we have ever had.

without fail—a demand or promise to do something
Be here at six A.M. without fail.
I will finish within three days without fail.

without ceremony—immediately and quietly
He took charge without ceremony and began to work.

that goes without saying—that is understood to be true
You will be paid well for your work; that goes without saying.

PART TWO:
PREPOSITIONS BY FUNCTION

BEFORE

—previous to a time
Ten o'clock is before eleven o'clock.

AFTER

—subsequent to a time
Three o'clock is after two o'clock.

DURING

—for part of a period
*He slept during the day. (He slept
from two P.M. until four P.M.)*
—at the same time as another event
She slept during the football game.

THROUGH, THROUGHOUT

—for an entire period, and after
*He slept through the day. (He slept
from 9 A.M. until 9 P.M.*

He slept throughout the day.

AT AROUND, AT ABOUT

—at an approximate time
We will leave at around six.
We will get there at about seven.

BY

—no later than a time
We have to be there by seven-fifteen.
by the time—when
*By the time you get here, we will
have left.*

TO, OF

—minutes before the hour
It's ten to four.
It's ten of four.

TOWARDS

—nearing a period of time
It was towards evening when she called.

BETWEEN

—after a time, and before another time
They will arrive between five and six.

WITHIN

—between now and a length of time
They will be here within ten minutes.

BEYOND, PAST

—after a time
Our guests stayed beyond midnight.
Our guests stayed past midnight.

UNTIL

—up to, but not after a time
The party will last until ten.

FOR

—during a length of time
They have been here for a week.

SINCE

—between a past time and now
They have been here since last Thursday.

IN

in time—not too late for an event
Try to get here in time to help me.

—a century, decade, year, season, month
He lived in the sixteenth century.
That singer was popular in the eighties.
We came here in the fall.

ON

on time—at the required time
He is punctual; he always arrives on time.
on the dot—at the exact minute
Be here at ten o'clock on the dot.

—a day, days, a date, dates
She is coming on Monday.
She doesn't work on Tuesdays.
I heard that singer on my birthday.

We came here in October.
We came here in 1997.
—after a length of time
She will be here in two weeks.

in the morning, afternoon, evening
They work in the morning.
He comes home in the afternoon.
We are going to go out in the evening.

We came here on October sixth.
We came here on October 6, 1997.

AT

at night
He works at night.
—a specific time
He comes home at ten o'clock.
at present—now
We are studying at present.
at the moment—now
I am not working at the moment.

WITH

—at the same time as
She wakes up with the sun.

OUT OF

to be out of time—to have no time left
We didn't finish, and now we are out of time.
to run out of time—use up remaining time.
We didn't eat because we ran out of time.

AHEAD OF

to be ahead of time—to be early

I'm glad you got here ahead of time; you can help me get ready for the party.

UP

time is up—there is no official time remaining for a specific activity.
I sat down when the bell rang because my time was up.

EXERCISE 1

Write the correct preposition in each blank:

1. Their daughter was born _____ 1998

   _____ October

   _____ the 18th

   _____ four-thirty

   _____ the afternoon.

2. I haven't seen my friend _____ August.

3. He was here _____ two weeks.

4. The play starts _____ seven o'clock _____ the dot, so be sure to be here _____ six-fifty.

5. Her mother is going to be here _____ the tenth _____ July. She will be here _____ two weeks.

6. Our neighbors always have a party _____ New Year's Eve. It usually starts

   _____ ten o'clock and lasts _____ the next morning.

7. Some people never go out _____ night because they get up so early _____ the morning.

8. Four o'clock is _____ five o'clock.

9. The baby didn't sleep _____ the night because he was so hungry.

10. I heard a noise _____ the night, but I was too sleepy to get up.

11. _____ the moment we are trying to study.

12. Some of us couldn't finish the test because the time was _____.

LOCATION

IN	ON	AT
—a continent, a country, a state, a city, a town	—a street, a floor	—a building, a house or apartment number
She lives in California.	*She lives on Oak Street.*	*She lives at The Manor.*
She lives in San Francisco.	*She lives on the fourth floor.*	*She lives at 1260 Oak Street.*
		at home—in one's own house
		at work—at one's job
		at school—attending school
		at church—attending church services
—a room, an area of a room	—an outside area	—a work area inside
She is in the kitchen, in the corner.	*He is standing on the corner.*	*She is at the kitchen sink.*
Our theater seats are in the balcony.	*He has an outdoor grill on the balcony.*	
—a comfortable chair	—a straight chair, a sofa, a couch	
He sat in the chair and watched television.	*He sat on the chair and ate his dinner.*	
	We sat on the sofa and watched television.	
in bed—under the covers	**on the bed**—on top of the covers	
—the water, the air, the environment	—facing a coast, a beach	—the coast, the beach
They are swimming in the water. There is pollution in the air.	*The house is on the beach.*	*The whole family is at the beach.*
—the center, the middle	—the side, left, right, surface	—the beginning, start, end
Our house is in the center of town.	*Our house is on the left side of the street.*	*Our house is at the end of the street.*
—the north/south/east/west	—the north side/south side/east side/west side	
New England is in the north of the United States.	*Our house is on the south side of town.*	
—a bodily attack	—the surface of the body	
The stone hit me in the face.	*He has a scratch on his arm.*	
—a vehicle one cannot walk around in (car/small boat/small plane/helicopter)	—a vehicle one can walk around on (bus/train/large boat/airplane)	
Please ride in the car with us.	*Please ride on the bus with us.*	
	—an individual vehicle (horse, bicycle, motorcycle, skates)	
	He came over on his bike.	

ABOUT, AROUND, THROUGHOUT

—in all areas of a place

The clothes were thrown about the room.

The papers were lying around the house.

There was trash throughout the house.

WITH

—in the same place as someone or something else

The baby is with the nurse.

I'm going to put my bag with yours on the chair.

ACROSS

—in all areas of a flat surface

The toys were scattered across the floor.

OVER, ABOVE

The white box is **over** the black box.
The white box is **above** the black box

BELOW, BENEATH, UNDER, UNDERNEATH

The black box is **below** the white box.
The black box is **beneath** the white box.
The black box is **under** the white box.
The black box is **underneath** the white box.

AGAINST

Chair A is **against** Chair B.

BY, BESIDE, NEXT TO

Chair B is **by** Chair C.
Chair B is **beside** Chair C.
Chair B is **next to** Chair C.

BETWEEN

Chair 2 is **between** Chair 1 and Chair 3.

AMONG

The black spot is **among** the white spots.

ON, ON TOP OF, UPON

The white lamp is **on** the table.
The white lamp is **on top of** the table
The white lamp is **upon** the table.

OFF

The black lamp is **off** the table.

IN, INSIDE, WITHIN

Apple A is **in** the box.
Apple A is **inside** the box.
Apple A is **within** the box.

OUT OF, OUTSIDE OF

Apple B is **out of** the box.
Apple B is **outside of** the box.

ACROSS FROM, OPPOSITE   IN FRONT OF, AHEAD OF   IN BACK OF, BEHIND

A   B   C

Chair C is **across from** Chair B.

Chair C is **opposite** Chair B.

Chair B is **in front of** Chair A.

Chair B is **ahead of** Chair A.

Chair A is **in back of** Chair B.

Chair A is **behind** Chair B.

NEAR, CLOSE TO   FAR FROM   BEYOND

A   B   C   D

Chair A is **near** Chair B.

Chair A is **close to** Chair B.

Chair C is **far from** Chair B.

Chair D is **beyond** Chair C.

AT THE TOP OF   AT THE BOTTOM OF

The X is **at the top of** the box.

The Z is **at the bottom of** the box.

ON THE TOP OF   ON THE BOTTOM OF   ON THE SIDE OF

The number 6 is **on the top of** the box.

The number 2 is **on the bottom of** the box.

The X and the Z are **on the sides of** the box.

EXERCISE 2
Write in the correct prepositions
A. Where is the star?

1. _____ the box

2. _____ the box

3. _____ the box

4. _____ the box

5. _____ the box

6. _____ the box

7. _____ the box

8. _____ the box

9. _____ the box

10. _____ the box

11. _____ the boxes

12. _____ the boxes

B. Her apartment is _____ Florida,

_____ Miami,

_____ The Palms

_____ Ocean Drive

_____ number 407.

She lives _____ the fourth floor

_____ a very nice apartment.

She is often _____ school

or _____ work.

When she is _____ home, she is usually asleep _____ bed.

However, right now she is

_____ the kitchen,

_____ the stove, cooking.

Soon she will sit down

_____ a dining room chair

_____ the table

_____ the corner, to eat her dinner.

She will probably be out

_____ the balcony after dinner,

sitting _____ a comfortable chair and relaxing.

ACROSS

The line goes **across** the box.

ALONG, BY

The line goes **along** the box.
The line goes **by** the box.

PAST

The line goes **past** the box.

THROUGH

The line goes **through** the box.

AROUND

The line goes **around** the box.

TO, TOWARD

The solid line goes **to** the box.
The dotted line goes **toward** the box.

FROM, AWAY FROM

The line goes **from** the box.
The line goes **away from** the box.

BACK TO

The line goes **back to** the box.

BACK FROM

The dotted line comes **back from** the box.

IN, INTO

The line goes **in** the box.
The line goes **into** the box.

OUT OF

The line goes **out of** the box.

ONTO

The line goes **onto** the table.

OFF

The line goes **off** the table.

OVER

The line goes **over** the hill.

DOWN

The line goes **down** the hill.

UP

The line goes **up** the hill.

WITH

The boat sails **with** the wind.

FOR

Spain

The plane is leaving **for** Spain.

U.S.A.

EXERCISE 3
Where is the dotted line going?

1. _____the box

2. _____the box

3. _____the box

4. _____the box

5. _____the box

6. _____the box

7. _____the box

8. _____the box

9. _____the box

10. _____the box

11. _____the box

12. _____the box

13. _____the box

14. _____the table

15. _____the table

About, around, above, over, under, and between are <u>adverbs</u> when used before numbers.

ABOUT, AROUND

approximately
There were about 200 people there.
There were around 200 people there.

ABOVE, OVER

more than
She has over a hundred books on that subject.
She has above a hundred books on that subject.

UNDER

less than
The car costs under a thousand dollars. **$895**

BETWEEN

higher than one number and lower than another
The tickets will cost between twenty and twenty-five dollars. **$21.50**

PLUS

indicates addition
Five plus six equals eleven. **$5 + 6 = 11$**

FROM

indicates subtraction
Three from ten equals seven. **$10 - 3 = 7$**

BY

indicates multiplication
Three multiplied by four equals twelve. **$3 \times 4 = 12$**

INTO

indicates division
Three into twelve equals four. $$3\overline{)12}^{\,4}$$

indicates a fraction

One-half of twelve is six.	1/2 x 12 = 6
One-third of nine is three.	1/3 x 9 = 3
Three-quarters of twelve is nine.	3/4 x 12 = 9

indicates all, part, or none of a specific plural or noncount noun, following **all, many, much, a lot, lots, plenty, enough, several, some, a few, a little, a bit, none**

All of the books on the table are yours.
Some of the money went to charity.
None of the furniture is valuable.

EXERCISE 4

Fill in each blank with the appropriate word:

1. He has (approximately) _____ 500 dollars in cash.

2. There are (more than) _____ twenty-five people here.

3. I paid (less than) _____ ten dollars for this meal.

4. The number six is _____ one and twelve.

5. 7 + 4 = 11   Seven _____ four equals eleven.

6. 12 − 2 = 10   Two _____ twelve equals ten.

7. $2\overline{)12}$ with 6 above   Two _____ twelve equals six.

8. One-tenth _____ one hundred equals ten.

DURING	IN	ON
—weather events (a storm, flood, hurricane, tornado, earthquake)	—types of weather (good, bad, foul, stormy cloudy, humid, wet, dry, hot, cold, sticky) **in the rain** **in the snow**	—types of days, periods of the day (nice days, sunny mornings, humid nights, rainy weekends)
We stayed at home during the storm.	*They swim in good weather.* *He walked home in the rain.* *The children played in the snow.*	*I sit on the balcony on sunny mornings.* *We play cards on rainy weekends.*

EXERCISE 5

Fill in the blanks with the correct prepositions:

1. I don't like to go out _____ bad weather.

2. The children love to play _____ the snow.

3. They have to stay inside _____ the storm.

4. We often go to the beach _____ sunny days.

5. She loves to walk _____ the rain.

6. She gets depressed _____ rainy days.

7. _____ the hurricane we stayed in the basement.

8. _____ cold days you have to wear a warm coat, a hat, and gloves.

9. _____ cold weather it is nice to sit by the fire.

10. What do you do _____ snowy evenings?

SOURCE OF INFORMATION

IN	ON
—written material (book, magazine, article, newspaper)	—electronically (the radio, the Internet, the telephone, television)
I read it in a book.	*I heard it on the radio.*
She found the article in a magazine.	*They saw him on television.*

EXERCISE 6

Fill in each blank with the appropriate preposition:

1. I saw your picture _____ the newspaper.

2. He found the information _____ the Internet.

3. She heard the news _____ television last night.

4. We looked up your number _____ the telephone directory.

5. I read that _____ a book.

6. He found those dates _____ an encyclopedia.

7. We watched that show _____ television.

8. The article was _____ a magazine.

9. There was a good program _____ the radio yesterday.

10. Did you talk to her _____ the telephone?

IN	OF	ON
—part of a group (association, bureau, category, choir, chorus, clan, club, division, family, fraternity, group, office, organization, society, sorority, union, political party)	—related to origin of place, time, culture, generation, race, religion, sex	—part of an exclusive group (board, committee, jury, panel, team, council, crew, faculty, honor roll, list, payroll, squad, staff)
The children in that family are all good students.	*The people of that city are very friendly.*	*The women on that committee are snobs.*
	—a special member of a group	
	She is the president of the college.	

EXERCISE 7

Fill in the blanks with the appropriate prepositions:

1. She is _____ the female sex.

2. My sister is _____ the jury.

3. She is also _____ the women's chorus.

4. Her son is _____ the softball team.

5. His wife is _____ a different religion.

6. Is your brother _____ a fraternity at college?

7. She was the president _____ the senior class.

8. I think her cousin is _____ the school board.

9. She is _____ the garden club.

10. They are going to put you _____ the payroll next month.

ABOUT	ABOVE	LIKE	OF	WITH
—partially describing	—better than	—similar to	—having an unseen characteristic	—having a physical characteristic
There is something cute about him. I don't see anything funny about that.	*He is above deceit. She is above cheating.*	*He is (just) like his father. He looks like his father.*	*She is a woman of honor. They are people of low morals.*	*I'm looking for a woman with red hair. He is the man with the broken arm.*

EXERCISE 8

Fill in the blanks with the appropriate prepositions:

1. He is _____ his brother.

2. She may be nasty, but she is _____ cruelty.

3. We don't know anything _____ that.

4. His reputation is spotless; he is a man _____ decency.

5. There is something special _____ him.

6. She's a little crazy, but there is something _____ her that I like.

7. Have you seen a man _____ white hair and glasses? I can't find my father.

8. He is very polite; he is a man _____ good manners.

9. I don't know anybody _____ him.

10. My friend is the girl _____ curly red hair.

(Dressed) IN	WITH ... ON	HAVE ... ON
He was dressed in black.	*He is the man with the black suit on.*	*The man has a black suit on.*
She came in a red dress.	*She is the lady with the red dress on.*	*The lady has a red dress on.*
They are always in jeans.	*They are the students with jeans on.*	*The students have jeans on.*

EXERCISE 9

Fill in the blanks with the appropriate words:

1. The lady was dressed _____ red.

2. The lady had a red suit _____.

3. The lady _____ the red suit _____ is my sister.

4. The children who _____ blue jackets _____ are my nephews.

5. The children were _____ blue jackets.

6. The children had blue jackets _____.

7. I saw a man _____ black.

8. I saw a man _____ a black hat _____.

9. I saw a man who had _____ a black hat.

10. The students are always dressed _____ jeans.

Prepositions after Verbs:

ABOUT		AT	IN	OF	ON	OVER
advise	know	aim	assist	advise	agree	argue
agree	laugh	glare	bask	complain	concentrate	battle
argue	lie	grab	cooperate	dream	expound	cry
ask	pray	hit	drown	hear	focus	fight
bother	question	laugh	help	inform	harp	grieve
brag	read	look	interest	know	insist	puzzle
care	remind	rush	invest	learn	report	sigh
complain	say	shoot	participate	remind	speak	worry
contact	sing	snatch	persist	sing	write	
cry	speak	stare	steep	speak		
do	talk	swing	submerge	talk		
dream	teach			tell		
fight	tell			think		
forget	think					
grieve	wonder					
harass	worry					
hear	write					
inform	yell					
joke						

EXERCISE 10

Fill in the blanks with the appropriate prepositions:

1. She advised me _____ my schedule.

2. We argued _____ money.

3. They don't know anything _____ cars.

4. He helped us _____ getting a loan.

5. He taught me a lot _____ music.

6. They insisted _____ leaving early.

7. Are you going to invest _____ that business?

8. What are you looking _____?

9. Why did he persist _____ asking that question?

10. The girl is going to report _____ the environment.

11. One shouldn't cry _____ spilled milk.

12. We all tried to participate _____ the discussion.

13. Everybody laughed _____ him when he put on that silly hat.

14. I am dreaming _____ a vacation at the beach.

15. The children are fighting _____ the toys.

16. What subjects are you interested _____?

17. They are aiming _____ very high goals.

18. She reminds me _____ her sister.

19. He is totally focused _____ his job.

20. It's too bad they lied _____ it.

FOR

usually indicates benefit
to recipient

after verbs:
bake, build, buy, cook, create,
dance, design, do, get, make,
play, sing, want something, win,
work, write

I wrote this poem for you.

after nouns:
advice, answer, cure, gift
help, idea, information, job,
present, something, surprise
letter, message, news, nothing,
plan, project, question, secret

Here is an answer for him.

indicates effect on recipient

after adjectives:
bad, beneficial, better,
crucial, good, harmful, healthy,
helpful, important, necessary,
unacceptable, unfavorable,
unhealthy, unimportant, useful,
worse

*That environment is unhealthy
for you.*

ON

Expressions:
have pity/mercy
*Please have pity on them.
The boss had mercy on us
and let us go home early.*

pull a gun/knife on
*The thief pulled a gun on
the frightened workers.*

TO

usually indicates transfer
to recipient

after verbs:
award, bring, carry, dedicate,
deliver, describe, devote,
distribute, donate, explain,
give, hand, introduce, lend,
mention, pass, present, read,
recommend, reveal, send,
shout, show, sing, speak,
submit, suggest, take, tell,
write

I wrote this letter to you.

after nouns:
answer, award, bill, dedication,
gift, letter, memorial,
monument, present, plaque,
remark, scholarship, statement,
toast

They gave the answer to him.

indicates effect on recipient

harmful
helpful
useful
beneficial
detrimental
unfavorable

*His advice was very useful
to her.*

indicates recipient's feelings

after adjectives:
abhorrent, acceptable,
annoying, boring, confusing,
crucial, distasteful, disturbing,
fascinating, gratifying, hurtful,
important, meaningful,
obnoxious, pleasing, precious,
preferable, repulsive, satisfying,
unacceptable, unimportant,
vexing, worrisome

*Those comments were
hurtful to us.*

EXERCISE 11

Fill in the blanks with the appropriate prepositions:

1. I hope they give the award _____ him.

2. She cooked a big meal _____ us.

3. The police had mercy _____ the young hooligans and sent them home.

4. The travel agency had a lot of information _____ her.

5. They sent a lot of information _____ her.

6. The information was useful _____ her.

7. This fresh fruit is good _____ you.

8. The news was fascinating _____ him.

9. Is the contract acceptable _____ you?

10. Practicing is very good _____ me.

11. They prepared a wonderful surprise _____ her.

12. Is television harmful _____children?

Nouns after Prepositions

AT	IN		ON	OUT OF	UNDER
attention	a hurry	disarray	a roll	breath	consideration
ease	a mess	disaster	approval	commission	construction
leisure	a mood	disgrace	board	control	discussion
peace	a rage	disorder	call	danger	investigation
play	a stew	doubt	course	focus	suspicion
rest	anguish	dread	display	gear	
risk	awe	fear	duty	luck	
war	bankruptcy	focus	edge	order	
work	captivity	gear	fire	practice	
	chaos	good health	guard		
	charge	jail	high/low volume		
	check	luck	high/low speed		
	circulation	hot water	hold		
	comfort	love	leave		
	commission	need	loan		
	condition	order	one's best behavior		
	confinement	pain	order		
	conflict	power	parole		
	confusion	ruins	record		
	control	session	sale		
	danger	shape	schedule		
	debt	sickness	stand-by		
	demand	tears	strike		
	despair	trouble	tap		
			target		
			track		
			trial		
			vacation		

EXERCISE 12

Fill in the blanks with the appropriate prepositions:

1. The children were _____ breath when they finished the game.

2. The new houses are _____ construction.

3. She is _____ a big hurry.

4. The soldiers stood _____ attention.

5. All of the workers are _____ strike.

6. They sat there _____ comfort all afternoon.

7. I'm afraid she's _____ a lot of trouble.

8. He isn't here; he's _____ vacation.

9. These CDs are _____ sale this week.

10. The poor man was _____ pain.

11. I hope your parents are _____ good health.

12. We were talking on the phone and he put me _____ hold.

13. That car seems to be _____ control.

14. Our boss is _____ control of the situation.

15. Both boys are _____ investigation.

SEPARATION

FROM	OF	OFF	OUT OF	WITH
after verbs: drive, keep, move, run, separate, stay, subtract, walk	**after verbs:** cure, die, relieve, rid	**after verbs:** break, chop, cut, pick, pull, saw, send, shave, take, tear, throw	**after verbs:** come, drive, get, go, grab, move, pour, pull, push, rip, sip, squeeze, take, tear	**after verbs:** be finished, be through, break up, cut ties, fall out, part, part company, sever relations, split up
after adjectives: divorced, separated	**after adjectives:** cured, relieved, rid			

EXERCISE 13

Fill in the blanks with the appropriate prepositions:

1. I'm glad you finally got rid _____ that old car.

2. He drove _____ the garage in a big hurry.

3. Are you finished _____ that project yet?

4. She walked _____ school to her apartment every day.

5. They relieved her _____ all her important duties.

6. They are going to send their children _____ to camp for the summer.

7. We can't move into the office until they move _____ it.

8. Before doing the laundry, I want to separate the dark clothes _____ the white ones.

9. Have you seen Sally? She has cut _____ all her hair!

10. It is wonderful; he has been cured _____ cancer.

Adjectives before Prepositions

ABOUT	AT	BY	FOR	IN	OF	TO	WITH
angry	aghast	amazed	eager	disappointed	afraid	addicted	annoyed
anxious	amazed	amused	concerned	interested	ashamed	committed	bored
bashful	amused	annoyed	grateful*		disrespectful	dedicated	content
concerned	angry	bewildered	prepared		envious	devoted	delighted
confused	annoyed	bored	ready		fond	faithful*	disappointed
crazy	astonished	confused	sorry		in favor	grateful*	disgusted
excited	astounded	disgusted			jealous	opposed	fascinated
faithful*	indignant	embarrassed			mindful		frustrated
glad	shocked	fascinated			proud		happy
happy	speechless	frustrated			repentant		impressed
honest	surprised	irritated			respectful		irritated
mad	thrilled	shocked			sure		pleased
nervous	upset				suspicious		satisfied
objective					scared		thrilled
optimistic					sure		unhappy
pessimistic					terrified		upset
right					tired		
sad					trusting		
sick					uncertain		
silly					unsure		
sorry					wary		
unhappy							
upset							
worried							

*grateful *to* a person/grateful *for* a thing
faithful *to* a person/faithful *about* doing something

EXERCISE 14

Fill in the blanks with the correct prepositions:

1. She is ashamed _____ her sloppy work.
2. Are you ready _____ the test?
3. We are grateful _____ you.
4. We are grateful _____ your help.
5. He is very annoyed _____ me.
6. Try to be objective _____ it.
7. They were shocked _____ the child's behavior.
8. I am interested _____ studying there.
9. He seems to be suspicious _____ us.
10. She is a little unsure _____ herself.

11. I am so pleased _____ the new house.

12. Was he embarrassed _____ the gossip?

13. We are optimistic _____ the future.

14. The students were not prepared _____ the exam.

15. She seems to be unhappy _____ something.

Adjectives before Prepositions

OF someone	ABOUT something	WITH something or someone else	TO someone else	TOWARD someone else	ON someone else
bad	careless	awkward	charming	affectionate	easy
careless	charming	belligerent	considerate	charitable	hard
charming	crazy	careful	courteous	considerate	rough
crazy	cruel	careless	cruel	cool	soft
crude	good	clumsy	faithful	courteous	strict
cruel	honest	curt	friendly	friendly	tough
evil	kind	flexible	good	gracious	
good	mean	forthcoming	gracious	hospitable	
hateful	nasty	frank	hateful	inhospitable	
honest	nice	friendly	helpful	menacing	
ignorant	rude	generous	hospitable	spiteful	
irresponsible	selfish	honest	inhospitable	sympathetic	
kind	sweet	impatient	kind	thoughtful	
mean	thoughtful	open	mean	warm	
nasty	thoughtless	patient	nice		
nice	understanding	stiff	polite		
responsible	unkind	sympathetic	rude		
rude		truthful	sweet		
selfish			sympathetic		
sweet			truthful		
thoughtful			unkind		
thoughtless					
typical					
unconscionable					
understanding					
unkind					

EXERCISE 15A

Fill in the blanks with the correct prepositions:

1. She was impatient _____ us.

2. He was rude _____ our absence.

3. Try to be courteous _____ everyone.

4. The teacher is too hard _____ him.

5. Thank you for being so hospitable _____ my mother.

6. They have been very sympathetic _____her.

7. The old man was generous _____ his money.

8. Do you think he is being honest _____ us?

9. She is faithful _____ her husband.

10. The landlord was nasty _____ my late payment.

Verbs before Prepositions

AT	ON	TO	TOWARD	WITH
cheer	center	adapt	contribute	agree
grumble	concentrate	admit	donate	collaborate
guess	dote	agree	give	comply
hint	dwell	appeal	go	concur
hoot	err	consent	head	cooperate
laugh	harp	listen	help	empathize
rebel	pick	object	lean	get along
rejoice	prey	pay attention	push	harmonize
snort	put pressure	react	take steps	help
tremble	wait	relate	work	negotiate
	work	reply		sympathize
		respond		work
		revert		
		subscribe		

EXERCISE 15B

Fill in the blanks with the correct prepositions:

1. He didn't respond _____ my letter.

2. You have to comply _____ the agreement.

3. We are working _____ our goals.

4. Try not to dwell _____ your problems.

5. I don't object _____ their coming.

6. They donated _____ several charities.

7. She is putting a lot of pressure _____ him.

8. I wish you wouldn't laugh _____ my mistakes.

9. They rejoiced _____ the news.

10. The children cried _____ delight.

Prepositions before Nouns

IN	WITH		IN/WITH	
assent	abandon	humility	anger	dread
cold blood	anger	indifference	apprehension	earnest
compliance	care	kindness	approbation	fairness
confusion	compassion	joy	approval	fear
consent	courage	love	compassion	friendship
defeat	delight	malice	confidence	gratitude
disgrace	despair	optimism	contempt	grief
disobedience	discretion	pleasure	defiance	happiness
dissent	disdain	pride	delight	kindness
desolation	distress	regard	despair	pain
fun	enthusiasm	sadness	disappointment	relief
person	fear	shame	disbelief	sadness
private	feeling	skill	disdain	shame
public	glee	sympathy	disgust	sorrow
reaction	grace	tenderness	dismay	sympathy
someone's absence	gratitude	thanks	distress	trust
someone's presence	happiness	understanding		
	hatred			

EXERCISE 15C

Fill in the blanks with the correct prepositions:

1. He resigned _____ disgrace.

2. She performed her duties _____ grace.

3. She hung her head _____ sorrow.

4. I told you that _____ confidence.

5. You have to deliver it _____ person.

6. The woman was clearly _____ pain.

7. She does her work _____ skill.

8. Please don't talk so loud _____ public.

9. The matter must be treated _____ discretion.

10. She accepted the invitation _____ pleasure.

PART THREE: USING PREPOSITIONS

A prepositional phrase is a <u>preposition plus an object</u>.
There are three possible patterns:

preposition + noun
preposition + pronoun
preposition + verb + -ing

PREPOSITION + NOUN

Singular Nouns

NORMAL PATTERNS

<u>preposition</u>	+	<u>noun determiner</u>	+/–	(descriptive adjectives)	+	<u>singular common noun</u>
with		a				pen
with		a		red		pen
with		a		new red		pen

SINGULAR NOUN DETERMINERS: a/an, the, one, this, that, any, each, every, another, either, neither, my, your, his, her, its, our, their, Mary's (or any other possessive noun)

EXCEPTION

<u>preposition</u>	+	ø	+	<u>singular common noun</u>
in				bed
to				school

Singular Proper Nouns

<u>preposition</u>	+	ø	+	<u>proper noun</u>
with				Mary
for				Mr. Jones

EXERCISE 1A

Correct the mistakes in the following prepositional phrases. Write the correct phrases in the blank spaces.

1. with pen   _____

2. for other girl   _____

3. to Mary cousin   _____

4. without book   _____

5. from nice boy   _____

6. between Mary and other girl   _____

7. in the Mary's house   _____

8. for the another apple _____

9. next to tall boy _____

10. near the Mr. Johnson's house _____

Plural Nouns

NORMAL PATTERNS

preposition +/−	(noun determiner) +/−	(descriptive adjective) +	plural common noun
for			apples
for	the		apples
for		red	apples
for	the	red	apples

PLURAL NOUN DETERMINERS: the, two (or any higher number), these, those, any, no, either, neither, other, some, both, few, enough, plenty of, a lot of, lots of, many, all, my, your, his, her, its, our, their, Mary's (or any possessive noun)

A plural noun not preceded by a noun determiner indicates all of the group or in general.

Plural Proper Nouns

preposition +	the +	proper noun
for	the	Joneses
for	the	United States

EXERCISE 1B

Correct the mistakes in the following prepositional phrases. Write the correct phrases in the blank spaces.

1. for three apple _____

2. without friend _____

3. in United States _____

4. from many country _____

5. to a lots of places _____

6. except this exercises _____

7. with another friends _____

8. at plenty of store _____

9. by other teacher _____

10. from the Smith _____

Noncount Nouns

NORMAL PATTERNS

preposition	+/−	(noun determiner)	+/−	(descriptive adjective)	+	noncount noun
for						water
for		the				water
for				hot		water
for		this		hot		water

NONCOUNT NOUN DETERMINERS: the, this, that, any, no, either, neither, some, little, enough, a lot of, lots of, plenty of, much, all, my, your, his, her, its, our, their, Mary's (or any possessive noun)

A noncount noun not preceded by a noun determiner indicates all of the group or in general.

EXERCISE 1C
Correct the mistakes in the following prepositional phrases. Write the correct phrases in the blank spaces.

1. for these furnitures _____

2. for a fresh air _____

3. with a new jewelry _____

4. without many hot water _____

5. with a few machinery _____

6. of a sugar _____

7. by mails _____

8. with too many junk _____

9. for a meat _____

10. for three equipment _____

PREPOSITION + PRONOUN
An object pronoun may replace a noun object.

TO REPLACE	USE	
the speaker	**me**	The letter is for **me**.
the person addressed	**you**	The letter is for **you**.
one male person (John)	**him**	The letter is for **him**.
one female person (Mary)	**her**	The letter is for **her**.
one thing (a book)	**it**	The letter is about **it**.

the speaker + one or more others	**us**	The letter is for **us**.
the people addressed	**you**	The letter is for **you**.
more than one person (John and Mary)	**them**	The letter is for **them**.
more than one thing (books)	**them**	The letter is about **them**.

If there is more than one object after a preposition, always use the object pronouns:

The letter is for **us**.   The letter is for **you** and **me**.
The letter is for **us**.   The letter is for **him** and **me**.
The letter is for **us**.   The letter is for **her** and **me**.
The letter is for **us**.   The letter is for **them** and **me**.

The letter is for **you**.   The letter is for **you** and **him**.
The letter is for **you**.   The letter is for **you** and **her**.
The letter is for **you**.   The letter is for **you** and **them**.

The letter is for **them**.   The letter is for **him** and **her**.
The letter is for **them**.   The letter is for **her** and **him**.
The letter is for **them**.   The letter is for **him** and **them**.
The letter is for **them**.   The letter is for **her** and **them**.

EXERCISE 1D

Change the underlined nouns to pronouns:

1. She paid for the apples.   _____

2. He is excited about the car.   _____

3. Do you study with your classmates?   _____

4. The rug was made by my grandmother.   _____

5. She made it for my sister and me.   _____

6. We will give it to our children.   _____

7. She is very fond of that boy.   _____

8. They put the papers in the trashcan last night.   _____

9. Please don't step on the floor until it is dry.   _____

10. He hopes to get a call from Sam and Mary tomorrow.   _____

11. It won't be the same without David and Amy and you. _____

12. There has been a lot of tension between Susan and me. _____

13. She lives near John and me.   _____

14. They have been very kind toward Sarah and the boys. _____

15. She seems to be getting over her problems.   _____

PREPOSITION + VERB

A verb following a preposition should be in its <u>gerund</u> (basic verb + ing) form.

A pencil is used	for	**writing.**
We are excited	about	**going.**
They are happy	about	**coming.**
I am interested	in	**learning.**
She takes a nap	after	**eating.**
He is proud	of	**winning.**

Be careful with the word **to**. It may be a preposition or part of an infinitive.

To is a <u>preposition</u> after:

be accustomed to	She is accustomed to	**driving**	fast.
be used to	She is not used to	**driving**	in traffic.
look forward to	She is looking forward to	**driving**	home.
admit to	She admitted to	**driving**	my car.
opposed to	She is opposed to	**driving**	while drunk.
limited to	She is limited to	**driving**	during the day.

More examples:

I have to get accustomed <u>to getting</u> up early.
She isn't used <u>to working</u> all day.
The child admitted <u>to making</u> a mistake.
We are looking forward <u>to seeing</u> you soon.
They are opposed <u>to changing</u> the rules.
He is limited <u>to exercising</u> in the morning.

To plus a basic verb forms an <u>infinitive</u>, and is not a preposition.
Use **to + basic verb** after the following verbs:

agree, appear, ask, be supposed, decide, expect, have, hope, intend, need, offer, plan, pretend, promise, refuse, seem, want, would like, used

Examples:

He <u>agrees to help</u> with the arrangements.
She <u>appears to be</u> hurt.
They <u>asked to leave</u> early.
I <u>need to sleep.</u>
We <u>want to go</u> home.
Would you <u>like to play</u> tennis?

Be careful with the expressions <u>be used to</u> and <u>used to</u>.
—<u>be used to</u> + gerund means "be accustomed to."
I am used to working hard.
We are not used to working at night.

—used to + basic verb means "did in the past."
I used to work hard when I was in college.
We used to work at night, but now we work during the day.

EXERCISE 1E
Fill in the blanks with the correct form of the verb:

1. She has to decide between _____ (study) and _____ (work).

2. That machine is great for _____ (exercise) the leg muscles.

3. He saved a lot of money by _____ (take) the bus to work.

4. Are you used to _____ (drive) on the freeway?

5. We decided against _____ (buy) that house.

6. They tried to stop her from _____ (move) so far away.

7. I am tired of _____ (cook) and _____ (clean).

8. He is really good at _____ (play) the guitar.

9. She is very close to _____ (win) the race.

10. You had better eat something before _____ (take) the medicine.

Choose work or working to complete the following:

11. She isn't used to _____ on Sundays.

12. He used to _____ every night.

13. I am opposed to _____ tomorrow.

14. She is supposed to _____ tomorrow.

15. He admits to _____ too little.

16. He agrees to _____ tomorrow.

17. We promise to _____ next week.

18. He would like to _____ every day.

19. They look forward to _____ here.

20. She expects to _____ here.

21. I am limited to _____ here.

22. Have you decided to _____ here?

23. They aren't used to _____ every day.

A. Basic Sentences with *Be*

STATEMENT PATTERN:

subject	+	verb	+	preposition	+	object
The letter		is		to		John.
The letter		is		about		money.
The letter		is		from		Springfield.
The letter		is		from		Virginia.

YES/NO QUESTION PATTERN:

verb	+	subject	+	preposition	+	object?
Is		the letter		to		John?
Is		the letter		about		money?
Is		the letter		from		Springfield?
Is		the letter		from		Virginia?

INFORMATION QUESTION PATTERN:

question word	+	verb	+	subject	+	preposition?
Who(m)*		is		the letter		to?
What		is		the letter		about?
Where		is		the letter		from?
What state		is		the letter		from?
Which state		is		the letter		from?

***Whom** is used in writing and in formal speech. **Who** is used in conversation.

EXCEPTION:

The preposition <u>at</u> is not used with <u>where</u> or <u>what time</u>.

STATEMENTS:

The party is at my house.
The party is at ten o'clock.

QUESTIONS:

Where is the party?
What time is the party?

EXERCISE 2A
Write a question that is answered by the underlined word in each statement.

1. <u>Yes</u>, the letter is from my mother.

_____

2. <u>No</u>, I am not in Chicago.

_____

3. We are from <u>California</u>.

_____

4. They are from <u>San Francisco</u>.

_____

5. The picture is of <u>my sister</u>.

_____

6. The article is about <u>dieting</u>.

_____

7. The class is at <u>seven-thirty</u>.

_____

8. The concert is at <u>Memorial Stadium</u>.

_____

B. Basic Sentences with Other Verbs

STATEMENT PATTERN:

subject	+	verb	+	preposition	+	object
She		writes		to		John.
She		asks		about		money.
She		writes		from		Springfield.
She		writes		from		Virginia.

YES/NO QUESTION PATTERN:

auxiliary verb	+	subject	+	verb	+	preposition	+	object?
Does		she		write		to		John?
Does		she		ask		about		money?
Does		she		write		from		Springfield?
Does		she		write		from		Virginia?

INFORMATION QUESTION PATTERN:

question word	+	auxiliary verb	+	subject	+	verb	+	preposition?
Who(m)		does		she		write		to?
What		does		she		ask		about?
Where		does		she		write		from?
What state		does		she		write		from?
Which state		does		she		write		from?

EXCEPTION:

The prepositons <u>to</u> and <u>at</u> are not used with <u>where</u>.

STATEMENTS:

The letter is going to Chicago.
We are staying at the Forum Hotel.

QUESTIONS:

Where is the letter going?
Where are you staying?

EXERCISE 2B
Write a question that is answered by the <u>underlined</u> word in each statement.

1. She works in the <u>furniture</u> department.

   _____

2. He calls from <u>his office</u>.

   _____

3. <u>No</u>, he doesn't send e-mail to me.

   _____

4. He sends e-mail to <u>his boss</u>.

   _____

5. <u>Yes</u>, he drives through Washington.

   _____

6. He drives through <u>Washington</u>.

   _____

7. They talk about <u>the garden</u>.

   _____

8. They discuss it with <u>their neighbors</u>.

_____

9. He goes to <u>Europe</u> every summer.

_____

10. She makes cookies for <u>her children</u>.

_____

11. He works at <u>the airport</u>.

_____

12. He works at <u>four o'clock</u>.

_____

A question word often connects statements containing the verbs know, understand, wonder, ask, and tell with a noun clause (subject + verb combination).

introduction	+	question word	+	noun clause
I know				
I don't know				
Do you know		who		he is.(?)
I understand				
I wonder				
Ask him				
Tell us				

Basic Patterns for Prepositions in Noun Clauses:

A. CLAUSES WITH *BE*

introduction	+	question word	+		noun clause		
				subject	+ verb	+	preposition
I know		who(m)		the letter	is		to.
I know		what		the letter	is		about.
I know		where		the letter	is		from.
I know		what state		the letter	is		from.
I know		which state		the letter	is		from.

B. CLAUSES WITH OTHER VERBS

introduction	+	question word	+		noun clause		
				subject	+ verb (object)	+	preposition
I know		who(m)		she	writes letters		to.
I know		what		she	asks		for.
I know		where		she	writes		from.
I know		what state		she	writes		from.

EXERCISE 3
Complete each answer:

1. Where is she from?

    I don't know _____

2. Who(m) is he talking to?

    I don't know _____

3. What does she write with?

    I wonder _____

4. Who do they live with?

I will ask them _____

5. Who(m) is this letter for?

We know _____

6. What does he do that for?

I don't understand _____

7. What company does she work for?

She will tell me _____

8. Which bus is she coming on?

I will ask her _____

9. Who(m) does she write letters to?

I don't know _____

10. Which courses are you registered for?

I don't understand _____

An <u>adjective clause</u> can identify a noun. The clause comes right after the noun.

Basic Patterns for Prepositions in Adjective Clauses:

A. TO IDENTIFY A <u>PERSON</u>, AN ADJECTIVE CLAUSE CAN BEGIN WITH **WHO(M), THAT,** OR **Ø**:

person	+	introduction	+	*adjective clause*		
				subject +	verb (object) +	preposition
The man		who(m)		she	writes	to
The man		that		she	writes	to
The man		—		she	writes	to
The people		who(m)		we	live	with
The people		that		we	live	with
The people		—		we	live	with
The doctor		who(m)		I	ask	for
The doctor		that		I	ask	for
The doctor		—		I	ask	for

Make sure the adjective clause is right after the noun:

The man who(m) she writes to   *is my father.*
The people that we live with   *are nice.*
The doctor I always ask for   *isn't here.*

My father is   *the man who(m) she writes to.*
I really like   *the people that we live with.*
This is not   *the doctor I always ask for.*

B. TO IDENTIFY A <u>THING</u>, AN ADJECTIVE CLAUSE CAN BEGIN WITH **THAT** OR **Ø**.

thing	+	introduction	+	*adjective clause*			
				subject +	verb +	(object) +	preposition
the book		that		I	paid ten dollars		for
the book		—		I	paid		for
the house		that		they	are looking		at
the house		—		they	are looking		at
the cities		that		we	work		in
the cities		—		we	work		in

Be sure to put the adjective clause directly after the noun.

The book that I paid ten dollars for   *is great.*
The house they are looking at   *is expensive.*
The cities that we work in   *are far apart.*

I really like   *the book I paid ten dollars for.*
They might buy   *the house they are looking at.*
We love   *the cities we work in.*

EXERCISE 4

Combine each set of sentences into one sentence by forming an adjective clause.

1. The man is my father. She writes letters to him.

   _____

2. The house is beautiful. My friends are looking at it.

   _____

3. Those are the children. My daughter plays with them.

   _____

4. The teacher isn't here. We talked to her yesterday.

   _____

5. The piano is fabulous. He paid a lot of money for it.

   _____

6. I am looking for the boy. I gave five dollars to him.

   _____

7. She likes the neighbor. She goes to the movies with him.

   _____

8. I lost the bag. I put my money in it.

   _____

9. I found the jacket. I took my keys out of it.

   _____

10. He can't remember the street. He parked on it.

    _____

A <u>phrasal verb</u> is a verb followed by a preposition that narrows or changes the meaning of the verb. Learn the verb and the preposition together as one unit.

There are three types of phrasal verbs—
   <u>nonseparable</u>   <u>separable</u>   <u>intransitive</u>
Each has its own set of word-order patterns.

NONSEPARABLE COMBINATIONS
Example: <u>look for</u> means "search."
Word order:
The object—noun or pronoun—immediately follows the preposition.

Statement Pattern:

subject	+	verb-preposition	+	noun or pronoun
She		is looking for		John.
She		is looking for		him.

    Incorrect: ~~She looks John for.~~
                      ~~She looks him for.~~

Question Pattern 1: Use with <u>what</u>, <u>which</u>, <u>who(m)</u>, and <u>whose</u>.

question word	+	auxiliary verb	+	subject	+	verb	+	preposition?
What		are		you		looking		for?
Which book		were		you		looking		for?
Who(m)		are		you		looking		for?
Whose book		did		you		look		for?

Question Pattern 2: Use with <u>why</u>, <u>when</u>, and <u>how</u>.

question word	+	auxiliary verb	+	subject	+	verb-preposition	+	noun or pronoun
Why		are		you		looking	for	John?
When		did		you		look	for	him?
How long		have		you		been looking for		him?
Where		have		you		looked	for	him?

    Incorrect: ~~Why are you looking John for?~~
                      ~~Why are you looking him for?~~

Noun Clauses

Pattern 1: Use with <u>what</u>, <u>which</u>, <u>who(m)</u>, and <u>whose</u>.

introduction	+	question		+		noun clause	
		word +	(object)	subject	+	verb +	preposition
I don't know		what	book	you		are looking	for.
I don't know		which	book	you		are looking	for.
I don't know		who(m)		you		are looking	for.
I don't know		whose	book	you		are looking	for.

Pattern 2: Use with <u>why</u>, <u>where</u>, <u>when</u>, and <u>how</u>.

introduction	+	question word	+	subject	+	verb	+	preposition	+	object
I don't know		why		you		are looking		for		the book.
I don't know		where		you		have looked		for		it.
I don't know		when		you		looked		for		it.
I don't know		how		you		can look		for		it.

Adjective Clauses

Pattern 1:

subject	+	adjective clause						
		who(m) that ø	+	subject	+	verb +	preposition +	verb
The man		who(m)		he		was looking for		is my father.
The book		that		he		was looking for		is on the table.

Pattern 2:

subject	+	verb	+	object	+	adjective clause				
						who(m) that ø	+	subject +	verb +	preposition
I		see		the man		who(m)		you	are looking	for.
We		found		the book		that		you	were looking	for.

Examples of Nonseparable Combinations

act like, ask for
beg off, break into
call on, care about, care for, check into, come across, come after, count on
fall for, fall off
get around, get off, get in, get on, get over, get with
go for, go over, go through, go with
hear from, hear of

keep at, keep off, keep on
lay off, live for, live on, live through
look after, look at, look for, look into, look over, look through
pick at, pick on
run across, run by, run for, run into, run over
see through, see to, show through, stand by, stand for
take after

EXERCISE 5A
Rewrite each sentence, changing the noun object to a pronoun:

1. We asked for *the information*.

   _____

2. She is going to call on *Mary and Carolyn* next week.

   _____

3. They just got on *the bus to Chicago*.

   _____

4. I came across *some old family pictures*.

   _____

5. The policeman is coming after *you and Jessica*.

   _____

6. She ran into *some old friends* at the mall.

   _____

7. I am going to stand by *my friend*.

   _____

8. He just went through *all his papers*.

   _____

9. We are looking for *Jason's wallet*.

   _____

10. That boy takes after *his father*.

    _____

EXERCISE 5B
Write a question for each of the sentences in the previous exercise.

Example:

1. What did you ask for _____ ?

2. Whom _____ ?

3. Which bus _____ ?

4. What _____ ?

5. Who(m) _____ ?

6. Who(m) _____ ?

7. Who(m) _____ ?

8. What _____ ?

9. Whose _____ ?

10. Whom _____ ?

EXERCISE 5C
Use the phrasal verb and tense indicated to complete each sentence:

1. I don't know what you _____ .

    (look for, present progressive)

2. He asked me what I _____ .

    (go through, past progressive)

3. She didn't tell us which hotel she _____ .

    (check into, past perfect)

4. I want to know whom he _____ .

    (care about, present)

5. I wonder what office she _____ .

    (run for, present progressive)

EXERCISE 5D
Complete each sentence using an adjective clause:

1. He was looking for a book.

    This is the book _____ .

2. Somebody broke into a house on this street.

    Is that the house _____ ?

3. She hopes to hear from that company soon.

    What is the name of the company _____ ?

4. The teacher picks on that group of students.

That is the group of students _____.

5. I have never heard of that place.

That is a place _____.

SEPARABLE COMBINATIONS

Examples: cross out something—"delete something by marking it"
              look up somebody—"try to find information about somebody"

Word order:

A noun object may follow the preposition.

He crossed out the mistake.
She looked up her old friend.

A noun object may precede the preposition.

He crossed the mistake out.
She looked her old friend up.

A pronoun object may precede, but not follow, the preposition.

He crossed it out.
She looked him up.

Incorrect: He crossed out it.
               She looked up him.

Question Pattern 1:

question word	+	auxiliary verb	+	subject	+	verb	+	preposition	+	noun object?
Why		did		he		cross		out		the mistake?
Why		did		she		look		up		her friend?

Question Pattern 2:

question word	+	auxiliary verb	+	subject	+	verb	+	object	+	preposition?
Why		did		he		cross		the mistake		out?
Why		did		he		cross		it		out?
Why		did		she		look		her old friend		up?
Why		did		she		look		him		up?

Noun Clauses

Pattern 1: Use with <u>why</u>, <u>when</u>, <u>how</u>, and <u>where</u>

introduction	+	question word	+	subject	+	verb	+	*noun clause* preposition	+	noun object
I don't know		why		he		crossed		out		the mistake.
I don't know		when		he		crossed		out		the mistake.
I don't know		how		she		looked		up		her friend.
I don't know		where		she		looked		up		her friend.

Incorrect:
┌───┐
│ ~~I don't know why he crossed out it.~~ │
│ ~~I don't know how he looked up her.~~ │
└───┘

Pattern 2: Use with <u>why</u>, <u>when</u>, <u>how</u>, and <u>where</u>

introduction	+	question word	+	subject	+	verb	+	object	+	preposition
I don't know		why		he		crossed		the mistake		out.
I don't know		when		he		crossed		it		out.
I don't know		how		she		looked		her friend		up.
I don't know		where		she		looked		him		up.

Pattern 3: Use with <u>what</u>, <u>which</u>, <u>who(m)</u>, and <u>whose</u>

introduction	+	question word	+	object	+	subject	+	verb	+	preposition
I don't know		what				he		crossed		out.
I don't know		what		mistake		he		crossed		out.
I don't know		which		mistake		he		crossed		out.
I don't know		whom				she		looked		up.
I don't know		whose		name		she		looked		up.

Adjective Clauses

Pattern:

subject	+	verb	+	object	+	*adjective clause* that who(m) ø	+	subject	+	verb	+	preposition
This		is		the mistake		that		he		crossed		out.
This		is		the mistake				he		crossed		out.
He		is		the friend		whom		she		looked		up.
He		is		the friend				she		looked		up.

Examples of Separable Combinations:

ask out
blow down, blow out, blow up
break down, break in, break up
bring about, bring back, bring down, bring on, bring up
call back, call off, call up, carry out, carry through, check off, check out
cheer up, chew out, clean up, cross out, cut down, cut out
do in, do over, draw up, drop by, drop in, drop off
figure out, fill in, fill out, fill up, find out, follow through
get across, get back, get in, get off, get on, get out
give back, give out
hand in, hand out, hand over, hang up, have on, have over, hold up
keep on, keep up, kick around, kick out, kick over, knock out
leave out, let down, look over, look up
make up, mark down, mark up, mix up
name after
pass in, pass on, pass out, pass over, pass up
pay back, pick out, pick over, pick up, point out, pull off, pull over
put back, put down, put on, put off, put out
rip off, round off, run by, run down, run up
see through, set up, show around, show up, shut off, stand up, start over
take back, take down, take for, take in, take off, take on, take out, take over, take up
tear down, tear off, tear out, tear up, think over, think up, throw out, try on, try out
turn around, turn down, turn in, turn off, turn on, turn over, turn up
wake up, wash out, wear out, work out, wrap up, write down, write up

EXERCISE 5E
Rewrite each sentence, changing the underlined nouns to pronouns:

1. The wind blew down two trees.
   The wind blew them down.

2. The teacher came in and broke up the party.

_____

3. Don't bring up that subject.

_____

4. Are you going to call off the wedding?

_____

5. We will clean up the mess.

_____

6. I have to fill out these forms.

_____

7. She is trying to get the mud off her shoes.

_____

8. Did you give back <u>the money</u>?

_____

9. We looked up <u>your sister</u> in Pittsburgh.

_____

10. He always mixes up <u>the twins</u>.

_____

EXERCISE 5F
Rewrite each sentence two ways, changing the pronouns to the nouns indicated:

1. They looked it over. (the new house)
   <u>They looked the new house over.</u>
   <u>They looked over the new house.</u>

2. We are going to pass them in. (our papers)

   _____

   _____

3. He has to pay it back. (the money)

   _____

   _____

4. Did they kick her out? (Jennifer)

   _____

   _____

5. I hope she doesn't pass it up. (this opportunity)

   _____

   _____

Separable Combinations with an Additional Preposition

When another preposition is added to a separable combination, the object, noun, or pronoun always goes between the verb and the two prepositions.

Pattern: verb + noun/pronoun + preposition + preposition + noun

Example: to take out of—to remove something from within
   Statement: *He took <u>the money</u> out of his back pocket.*
                              He took <u>it</u> out of his pocket.

Question:	*What did he take the money out of?*
	Which pocket did he take it out of?

Noun Clause:	*I don't know which pocket he took the money out of.*
	I don't know which pocket he took it out of.

Adjective Clause:	*This is the pocket (that) he took the money out of.*
	This is the pocket he took it out of.

Example: to give back to—to return something to somebody

Statement:	We gave the letter back to her.
	We gave it back to her.

Question:	Who(m) did you give the letter back to?
	Who(m) did you give it back to?

Noun Clause:	I don't know who(m) we gave the letter back to.
	I don't know who(m) we gave it back to.

Adjective Clause:	She is the girl who(m) we gave it back to.
	She is the girl we gave the letter back to.

Examples of Separable Combinations with an Additional Preposition:

bring down on, bring up to
check out of
get back from, get out of, give back to
hand in to, hand out to, hand over to, hang up on
mix up with
run out of
take away from, take out of, tear out of
wash out of, write down on

EXERCISE 5G
Change each statement into a yes/no question. Change the underlined nouns to pronouns.

1. He brought the books up to the fourth floor.

   Did he bring them up to the fourth floor?

2. She is going to check some books out of the library.

   _____

3. He is trying to get the spot out of his shirt.

   _____

4. We got <u>our clothes</u> back from the dry cleaners.

_____

5. He is going to hand <u>his letter of resignation</u> in to the manager tomorrow.

_____

6. You should hang <u>your coat</u> up on the hanger.

_____

7. She mixes <u>the dough</u> up with her fingers.

_____

8. The police are going to run <u>the ruffians</u> out of town.

_____

9. She takes <u>the groceries</u> out of the car herself.

_____

10. I wrote <u>your number</u> down on a scrap of paper.

_____

INTRANSITIVE COMBINATIONS
Example: act up—"misbehave"
There is no object; the word following the verb is now an <u>adverb</u>.

Statement Pattern:
subject	+	verb	+	adverb
The child		acted		up

Question Pattern:
(question word)	+	auxiliary verb	+	subject	+	verb	+	adverb?
Why		did		the child		act		up?

Noun Clause Pattern:
introduction	+	question word	+	subject	+	verb	+	adverb
I don't know		why		the child		acted		up.

Adjective Clause Pattern:
subject	+	who that	+	verb	+	adverb	+	verb
The child		who		acted		up		is in the kitchen.

Examples of Intransitive Verb + Adverb Combinations:
act up, add up
back down, back off, back up, blow away, blow out, blow over, blow up
break down, break in, break out, break up, burn down, burn up, butt in
calm down, carry on, catch on, catch up, check in, check out, cheer up, chicken out
chip in, clam up, close down, close in, close out, close up
come about, come out, come through, come to, crack down, crop up, cut back
drag on, drop by, drop in, drop off, drop out
eat out
fall down, fall off, fall out, fall over, fall through, fill out, find out
get about, get along, get around, get away, get by, get off, get on, get out, get through, get up
give in, give up
go about, go by, go on, go out, go through
goof off, grow up
hang around, hang out, hang up, hear of
keep in, keep out, keep up, kick in
live on, look in, look out, luck out
make out, make up
nod off
pan out, pass away, pass out, pick up, pull over
run around

show up, slip up, stand by, stand out, stand up, start over
take off, take over, throw up, try out, turn in, turn out, turn up
wake up, watch out, work out

EXERCISE 5H

Rewrite each sentence, using an intransitve verb-adverb combination in place of the underlined verb.

1. The children <u>misbehaved</u>.

<u>The children acted up.</u>

2. I hope the boss doesn't <u>lose his temper</u> because we are late.

_____

3. The thieves <u>entered the building by force</u>.

_____

4. Please try to <u>be still and quiet</u>.

_____

5. Do you think they will <u>understand the rules quickly</u>?

_____

6. What time did you <u>fall asleep</u>?

_____

7. It is important to <u>become mature</u>.

_____

8. Those kids <u>act silly and do nothing</u> all day.

_____

9. <u>Do not trespass</u>!

_____

10. We passed the exam; we <u>were very fortunate</u>.

_____

Intransitive Verb-Adverb Combinations Followed by a Preposition

Example 1: to get along with—to live in harmony with
    Statement: ***She gets along with her roommates.***
                    She gets along with them.

    Question: ***Who(m) does she get along with?***

Noun Clause:	*It doesn't matter who(m) she gets along with.*
Adjective Clause:	*Those are the roommates [who(m)] she gets along with.*

Example 2: to get through with—to finish something that requires effort

Statement:	*They have to get through with their exams.* *They have to get through with them.*
Question:	*What do they have to get through with?*
Noun Clause:	*I don't care what they have to get through with.*
Adjective Clause:	*These are the exams (that) they have to get through with.*

Examples of Verb-Adverb-Preposition Combinations:

add up to
back down from, bone up on, break up with, brush up on
carry on with, catch on to, catch up with, chicken out on, close in on, come down on, come down with, crack down on, cut back on
drop in on, drop out of
face up to, fall in with, fall out of, feel up to, fill in for, find out about
get ahead of, get along with, get around to, get away from, get away with, get out of, get through with, give up on
go around with, go in for, go out for, go out with, go through with
hang around with, hang out with, hang up on
keep away from, keep up with
look back on, look down on, look in on, look out for, look up to
make up with
put up with
run around with, run out of
stand in for, stand up for, stand out from, start over from
take off from, take over from, try out for
watch out for, wear out from

EXERCISE 51
Rewrite each sentence, using a verb-adverb-preposition expression in place of the underlined words.

1. My sister is going to <u>stop dating</u> her boyfriend tonight.

   <u>My sister is going to break up with her boyfriend tonight.</u>

2. I don't understand how she <u>tolerates</u> her new roommate.

   _____

3. He is looking for another teacher to <u>substitute for</u> him tomorrow.

   _____

4. The doctor told her to <u>drink less</u> coffee.

_____

5. If you have a cold, you should <u>avoid</u> other people as much as possible.

_____

6. It is hard for the smaller children to <u>maintain the pace of</u> the big ones.

_____

7. We have to go to the store; we have <u>exhausted our supply of</u> milk for the baby.

_____

8. The children are <u>exhausted from</u> playing all day.

_____

9. They will have to <u>confront</u> the facts.

_____

10. We all <u>respect and admire</u> our boss.

_____

PHRASAL VERBS USED AS NOUNS

Many phrasal verbs are commonly used as nouns.
  There are three ways to write these nouns:
  —as two separate words
    Example: a **rip off**—a robbery
    I had to pay fifteen dollars to park my car. What a rip off!

  —with a hyphen between the two words
    Example: a **stand-in**—a substitute
    She worked as a stand-in when the manager was on vacation.

  —as one word
    Example: a **turnout**—the size of an audience
    We had a great turnout for our baseball game.

Unfortunately, there is no good rule or guideline to help us know which of the three forms to use. Many organizations have their own style manual to specify the usage they prefer.

Use these combinations as singular or plural nouns; use noun-determiners and descriptive adjectives as usual.

Examples of Phrasal Verbs Used as Nouns:

blowout—a tire that has burst
We had a blowout on the highway.

break-down—a collapse
Rioters crowded the streets and there was a general break-down of order.

break-in—an illegal or forced entry into a room or building
We had a break-in at the office last night; several computers were stolen.

break-up—a separation caused by disagreement
The young girl was unhappy about the break-up with her boyfriend.

come-on—an incentive
The free T-shirts at the game were a come-on to get more people to buy tickets.

cover up—an attempt to hide the truth
The cover-up of the crime made it difficult to investigate.

close-up—a photograph of someone's face
That photographer is very good at close-ups.

getaway—a vacation
That travel agency advertises exotic getaways.

giveaway—something that can be obtained for free
There were a lot of prizes and giveaways at the fair.

hand-me-down—clothing used first by an older child and later by a younger one
As the youngest child in a big family, almost all her clothes were hand-me-downs.

handout—free food or supplies
Many homeless people survive on handouts.

hang-up—a psychological problem
Her insecurity is one of her hang-ups.

hangout—a place where friends often go for relaxation or entertainment
The bar on the corner is their favorite hangout.

kickback—money received by a controlling agent in a business transaction
We believe somebody got a kickback in that business deal.

leftovers—food saved for another meal
We have leftovers for a week after a big holiday meal.

letdown—a return to normal life after a time of excitement
It was a big letdown for her to go back to work after her long vacation.

lookout—a place for observing the activities of others
The detective had a great lookout from the tenth floor of that building.

makeup—paint for the face
Most women look better with a little makeup.

mark-down—merchandise that has been reduced in price
The mark-downs are in the basement of the store.

mix-up—confusion caused by an error
There were a lot of mix-ups during our tour; most of the information we received about prices, hours of operation, and transportation was incorrect.

pullover—a sweater that you put on by pulling it over your head

Pullovers are comfortable and attractive.

pushover—a gullible person

Her husband is a pushover; he will buy anything from a slick salesman.

rip-off—a high price for something of lesser value

He paid too much for that antique chair; it was a rip-off.

show-off—a person who constantly demonstrates his talents

I don't like to dance with him because he is a big show-off.

stand-in—a substitute

The stand-in for the main actor did a great job.

step up—an improvement in status

The new house is a step up for him.

takeoff—departure of an airplane

The takeoff was smooth, but the landing was difficult.

takeover—the assumption of control, management, or responsibility of another group

There have been a lot of takeovers of big companies this year.

tryouts—auditions

If you want to be on the team, come to the tryouts tomorrow afternoon.

turnaround—a change in attitude

When he met her he went from depressed to cheerful; it was a complete turnaround.

turnout—the number of people attending an event

The turnout for the office picnic was great; almost everybody came.

workout—a session of exercise

A daily workout can improve your disposition.

write-up—an article in a newspaper or a magazine

There was a big write-up about our friend in last week's paper.

EXERCISE 5J
Write the appropriate nouns in the blanks.

1. Our tire burst on the highway. We had a _____.

2. My friend is going to a psychologist to try to get rid of her _____.

3. The beach is private and quiet; it is a perfect _____ for a busy couple.

4. The woman carefully applied lipstick, powder, and mascara; she was an expert at putting on _____.

5. She paid two thousand dollars for that old, broken-down car. What a _____!

6. That soccer player always gets the ball and dances around with it. He is a big

_____.

7. If you want to audition for the school chorus, come to the auditorium for

_____ on Thursday at four o'clock.

8. The kids always go there to relax after school. It's their favorite

_____.

9. Walking fast for an hour every day is a good _____.

10. Be sure to read the review of the show in the newspaper. It was an excellent

_____.

PHRASAL VERBS USED AS ADJECTIVES

Verb-preposition combinations are used as adjectives in some common expressions. When used as adjectives before nouns, these combinations are hyphenated.

check-out counter—the place where the cashier is located
   Please take all your purchases to the check-out counter.
drive-by shooting—a crime involving the indiscriminate use of a gun from a vehicle
   The wounded people were victims of a drive-by shooting.
carry-out/take-out food—food prepared and sold to be eaten somewhere else
   She lives alone, and thrives on carry-out food.
drive-in restaurant/movie; drive-through bank/carwash—a business where people enjoy the services without leaving their cars
   Drive-in movies were popular in the fifties, but not anymore.
hand-me-down clothes—used clothes
   In order to save money, the student wore hand-me-down clothes.
left-over food—prepared food saved from a previous meal
   Left-over food is never as good as it was when it was fresh.
run-down neighborhood—a neglected area
   There are too many run-down neighborhoods in the city.
stand-up comic—an entertainer who stands at a microphone and tells jokes
   He made quite a bit of money as a stand-up comic.
sit-down dinner/lunch/meal—a meal where the food is served at the table, rather than buffet style.
   They had a wonderful sit-down dinner at their wedding reception.
wake-up call—a telephone call ordered by a hotel guest to help him wake up
   Our plane is leaving early in the morning, so we will need a wake-up call.
wind-up toy—a mechanical toy that works by turning a key
   The children love to play with wind-up toys.

EXERCISE 5K

Fill in each blank with a verb-preposition combination used as an adjective:

1. You can pay for your groceries at the _____ counter.

2. I'm cooking dinner at home tonight; I'm really tired of _____ food.

3. Whenever I check into a hotel, I ask for a _____ call for the next morning.

4. The politicians promised to help clean up the _____ neighbor-hoods around the city.

5. It is very convenient to deposit your checks at a _____ bank.

In the following examples, a preposition has been added to the beginning of the original word, making it more specific.

NOUNS

by-line—a line at the beginning of an article with the author's name
His article was published, and he was pleased to see his name on the by-line.

bypass—a route that goes around a city, rather than through it
Taking the bypass saves a lot of time.
—a surgical operation that avoids the main organ
Her father had a heart bypass last month.

back-up—someone who can substitute if necessary
I think I am well enough to do the job; if not, my colleague is here as a back-up.

downgrade—a change to a lower quality
His new position is a downgrade in salary, but he is happier.

downpour—a heavy rain
The streets are flooded after that downpour yesterday.

downtown—the heart of a city
Let's go downtown tonight and have fun.

downswing—a reduction in business activity
There was a downswing in the first quarter of the year.

input—the contribution of ideas
We really need your input for this proposal.

off-chance—an unlikely possibility
He called me on the off-chance that I would be available.

off-shoot—a branch
That group is an off-shoot of a national organization.

outbreak—an eruption
There has been an outbreak of the flu in this city.

outlaw—a criminal
The cowboy films always have heroes and outlaws.

outpost—a place of business far away from city life
His store is a little outpost in the middle of nowhere.

outpouring—an abundance
There was an outpouring of sympathy for the widow.

output—production
Our output for the month was huge; we made a lot of money.

overkill—failure caused by too much effort
The salesman talked so much that the client lost interest; it was complete overkill.

overpass—a bridge that extends over a road
An overpass is being built at that intersection; it will ease the traffic situation.

throughway—highway

You should go on the throughway; it's much faster.

underdog—the team or person not expected to succeed

It's exciting when the underdog wins in a tournament.

underpass—a road built underneath another road

To get on the main highway, you need to get on the underpass first.

underpinnings—foundation

If the underpinnings are strong, the building will be safe.

update—the latest information

The television stations are giving us an update on the tragedy every five minutes.

upheaval—a disruption

There is a big upheaval going on in our office; a lot of people are being transferred.

upstart—ambitious newcomer

The new assistant tried to change our office procedures during her first week. What an upstart!

upsurge—increase in activity

There was an upsurge during the second quarter, thank goodness!

upswing—increase in activity

There has been a steady upswing this year.

Certain expressions use prepositions in noun form.

the ins and outs—all of the details

After owning a restaurant for twenty years, he knows all the ins and outs of the business.

the ups and downs—the good things and the bad things

We learn to cope with the ups and downs of life.

EXERCISE 6A

Fill in each blank with a preposition-noun combination:

1. That business lost money during the _____ in August.

2. The arrival of tourists in the spring means a big _____ in business activity.

3. At the meeting they asked for _____ from everybody in the department.

4. Our boss gives us an _____ on the company's activities at the end of every month.

5. You'd better get a flu shot in case there is an _____ of the flu next winter.

ADJECTIVES

back-up—reserve

There is a back-up crew in case you need help.

bygone—past

In bygone days, the pace of life was slower.

downbeat—unhappy

He has been downbeat ever since his girlfriend left town.

for-profit—money-making

That group looks like a charity, but it is really a for-profit operation.

in-class—activity done in the classroom, rather than as homework

We have to write an in-class composition.

incoming—being received

The incoming mail should go in that pile.

off-color—obscene

I really hate his off-color remarks.

offshore—in the ocean or sea

They are trying to regulate the offshore drilling of oil.

off-the-cuff—spontaneous

Her off-the-cuff remarks prove her to be very well informed.

ongoing—currently in progress

Everyone is sick of the long ongoing investigation.

on-line—pertaining to the Internet

On-line services get better every day.

outgoing—extroverted

He is one of the most outgoing young people I have ever met.

out-of-the-way—far away, and not on the main road

He proposed to her at a romantic, out-of-the-way restaurant.

overdone—ruined from cooking too long

The dinner wasn't good; the meat was raw and the vegetables were overdone.

overextended—too busy

Her life is very stressful because of her overextended schedule.

overjoyed—very happy

He was overjoyed when he heard the news.

overpaid—receiving more money than one is worth

The organization has a few overpaid employees.

overbearing—domineering

Life is stressful when you have an overbearing boss.

underdone—not cooked long enough

The meat was underdone, so we put it back in the oven.

underpaid—paid less than one is worth

The workers at that factory are underpaid.

upbeat—in a good mood

Everybody is upbeat because of the holidays.

upmarket—stylish and expensive

The new mall has only upmarket shops; there are no discount stores there.

In the following expressions, prepositions are used in the form of adjectives:

the down side—the negative aspect

The down side of my new job is that I have to work on Saturdays.

the inside story—information known only by the people concerned

The tabloid newspapers always claim to have the inside story, but it is usually only speculation.

the in crowd/thing/place—what is currently popular

In high school, she was always part of the in crowd.

Body piercing was the in thing in the early nineties.

That nightclub is the in place for the over-thirty crowd.

the up side—the positive aspect

The up side of the new job is that there will be a lot of international travel.

EXERCISE 6B

Fill in each blank with a preposition-adjective combination with the indicated meaning:

1. We were _____ (thrilled) at the news.

2. She got the information through her _____ (Internet) contacts.

3. Many people are _____ (given too much work) and _____ (given very low wages).

4. Her new boyfriend is friendly and _____ (extroverted).

5. During the interview they explained the _____ (positive) side and the _____ (negative) side of working there.

VERBS

In the following examples, a preposition has been added to the beginning of a verb, giving it more specific meaning.

bypass—to go around a city to avoid the downtown traffic

If you are in a hurry, you can bypass Philadelphia by taking the alternate route.

downgrade—to lower in quality or status

They downgraded her job, so she is looking for another one.

download—to add software to a computer

She downloaded a new program this morning.

outdo—to surpass

She is very ambitious; she wants to outdo everybody.

outlaw—to make illegal

They have outlawed smoking in many public places.

outpace—to go faster

The men outpaced the boys right from the beginning of the race.

overcome—to conquer

She overcame her shyness and made a lot of friends.

overdo—to work too hard

After the operation, the doctor told him not to overdo it.

overtake—to reach and then surpass

We knew him when he was just learning to dance, but he overtook us and is now a professional.

overturn—to change from a negative situation to a positive one

There has been a big overturn in the school system.

overwhelm—to surprise in the extreme

The teacher was overwhelmed by the party the students gave in her honor.

undercut—to succeed by offering a lower price than one's competitors

Discount stores usually undercut the department stores.

update—the latest news

Do you have an update on the hurricane?

upgrade—to raise in quality or status

She is earning more money because they upgraded her job.

withdraw—to stop participating

It is a shame you have to withdraw from the class.

withhold—keep money that will be owed to you at a later date

The government withholds part of your salary for income tax.

In the following expressions, prepositions are used in the form of verbs.

to "up" something—to increase something

I wish I had bought that coat last year; they have upped the price.

The gym workout is getting easier; it's time to up the weights on the machines.

to "down" something—to drink something very fast

After the race, he downed four glasses of water.

EXERCISE 6C

Fill in each blank with an appropriate preposition-verb combination:

1. In an effort to save money, they are going to _____ (decrease the status of) a lot of jobs.

2. I hope they can _____ (conquer) all of their difficulties.

3. That team didn't have enough players and they had to _____ (cancel participation) from the tournament.

4. He bought her a huge diamond ring, hoping to _____ (surprise and impress) her.

5. Do you think they will ever _____ (prohibit) guns in this country?

PART FOUR: ANSWERS AND GLOSSARY

ANSWERS TO EXERCISES

Part Two

1.

1. in, in, on, at, in
2. since
3. for
4. at, on, by
5. on, of, for/in
6. on, at around/at, until
7. at, in
8. after
9. through/during
10. during
11. At
12. up

2A.

1. on
2. in
3. near
4. far from
5. over
6. in back of/behind
7. at the top of
8. at the bottom of
9. next to
10. against
11. between
12. among

2B.

in, in, at, on, at, on, in, at, at, at, in, in, at, on, at, in, on, in

3.

1. across
2. up
3. over
4. away from
5. out of
6. down
7. back to
8. into
9. toward
10. through
11. along
12. past
13. around
14. onto
15. off

4.

1. about
2. over
3. under
4. between
5. plus
6. from
7. into
8. of

5.

1. in
2. in
3. during
4. on
5. in
6. on
7. During
8. On
9. In
10. on

6.

1. in
2. on
3. on
4. in
5. in
6. in
7. on
8. in
9. on
10. on

7.

1. of
2. on
3. in
4. on
5. of
6. in
7. of

8. on
9. in
10. on

8.

1. like
2. above
3. about
4. of
5. about
6. about
7. with
8. of
9. like
10. with

9.

1. in
2. on
3. with, on
4. have, on
5. in
6. on
7. in
8. with, on
9. on
10. in

10.

1. about
2. about/over
3. about
4. in

5. about

6. on

7. in

8. at

9. in

10. on

11. over

12. in

13. at

14. of/about

15. over

16. in

17. at

18. of

19. on

20. about

11.

1. to

2. for

3. on

4. for

5. to

6. to/for

7. for

8. to

9. to

10. for

11. for

12. to/for

12.

1. out of

2. under

3. in

4. at

5. on

6. in

7. in

8. on

9. on

10. in

11. in

12. on

13. out of

14. in

15. under

13.

1. of

2. out of/from

3. with

4. from

5. of

6. off

7. out of

8. from

9. off

10. of

14.

1. of
2. for
3. to
4. for
5. at/with
6. about
7. at
8. in
9. of
10. of
11. with
12. about
13. about
14. for
15. about

15A.

1. with
2. about
3. to
4. on
5. to
6. to/with
7. with
8. with
9. to
10. about

15B.

1. to
2. with
3. toward
4. on
5. to
6. to
7. on
8. at
9. about
10. with

15C.

1. in
2. with
3. in
4. in
5. in
6. in
7. with
8. in
9. with
10. with

Part Three

1A.

1. with a pen
2. for a girl/for this girl/for that girl/for another girl
3. to Mary's cousin
4. without a book

5. from a nice boy

6. between Mary and another girl

7. in Mary's house

8. for another apple

9. next to a/the tall boy

10. near Mr. Johnson's house

1B.

1. for three apples

2. without friends

3. in the United States

4. from many countries

5. to lots of places/to a lot of places

6. except these exercises

7. with other friends

8. at plenty of stores

9. by other teachers

10. from the Smiths

1C.

1. for this furniture

2. for fresh air

3. with new jewelry

4. without much hot water

5. with a little machinery

6. of sugar

7. by mail

8. with too much junk

9. for meat

10. for equipment

1D.

1. them
2. it
3. them
4. her
5. us
6. them
7. him
8. it
9. it
10. him and her/them
11. you
12. her and me/us
13. us
14. them
15. them

1E.

1. studying, working
2. exercising
3. taking
4. driving
5. buying
6. moving
7. cooking, cleaning
8. playing
9. winning
10. taking
11. working
12. work

13. working

14. work

15. working

16. work

17. work

18. work

19. working

20. work

21. working

22. work

23. working

2A.

1. Is the letter from your mother?

2. Are you in Chicago?

3. Where are you from?/What state are you from?

4. What city are they from?

5. Who is the picture of?

6. What is the article about?

7. What time is the class?

8. Where is the concert?

2B.

1. What/Which department does she work in?

2. Where does he call from?

3. Does he send e-mail to you?

4. Who(m) does he send e-mail to?

5. Does he drive through Washington?

6. What city does he drive through?

7. What do they talk about?

8. Who(m) do they discuss it with?

9. Where does he go every summer?

10. Who(m) does she make cookies for?

11. Where does he work?

12. What time does he work?

3.

1. where she is from.

2. who(m) he is talking to.

3. what she writes with.

4. who(m) they live with.

5. who(m) this letter is for.

6. what he does that for.

7. what company she works for.

8. which bus she is coming on.

9. who(m) she writes letters to.

10. which courses I am registered for.

4.

1. The man [who(m)] she writes letters to is my father.

2. The house (that) my friends are looking at is beautiful.

3. Those are the children [who(m)] my daughter plays with.

4. The teacher [who(m)] we talked to yesterday isn't here.

5. The piano (that) he paid a lot of money for is fabulous.

6. I am looking for the boy [who(m)] I gave five dollars to.

7. She likes the neighbor [who(m)] she goes to the movies with.

8. I lost the bag (that) I put my money in.

9. I found the jacket (that) I took my keys out of.

10. He can't remember the street (that) he parked on.

5A.

1. We asked for it.

2. She is going to call on them next week.

3. They just got on it.

4. I came across them.

5. The policeman is coming after you.

6. She ran into them at the mall.

7. I am going to stand by him/her.

8. He just went through them.

9. We are looking for it.

10. That boy takes after him.

5B.

1. did you ask for?

2. is she going to call on?

3. did they just get on?

4. did you come across?

5. is the policeman coming after?

6. did she run into at the mall?

7. are you going to stand by?

8. did he just go through?

9. wallet are you looking for?

10. does that boy take after?

5C.

1. are looking for.

2. was going through.

3. had checked into.

4. cares about.

5. is running for.

5D.

1. he was looking for.

2. somebody broke into.

3. she hopes to hear from?

4. the teacher picks on.

5. I have never heard of.

5E.

1. The wind blew them down.

2. The teacher came in and broke it up.

3. Don't bring it up.

4. Are you going to call it off?

5. We will clean it up.

6. I have to fill them out.

7. She is trying to get it off her shoes.

8. Did you give it back?

9. We looked her up in Pittsburgh.

10. He always mixes them up.

5F.

1. They looked the new house over./ They looked over the new house.

2. We are going to pass our papers in./ We are going to pass in our papers.

3. He has to pay the money back./He has to pay back the money.

4. Did they kick Jennifer out?/Did they kick out Jennifer?

5. I hope she doesn't pass this opportunity up./I hope she doesn't pass up this opportunity.

5G.

1. Did he bring them up to the fourth floor?

2. Is she going to check them out of the library?

3. Is he trying to get it out of his shirt?

4. Did we get them back from the dry cleaners?

5. Is he going to hand it in to the manager tomorrow?

6. Should you hang it up?

7. Does she mix it up with her fingers?

8. Are the police going to run them out of town?

9. Does she take them out of the car herself?

10. Did I write it down on a scrap of paper?

5H.

1. The children acted up.

2. I hope the boss doesn't blow up because we are late.

3. The thieves broke in.

4. Please try to calm down.

5. Do you think they will catch on?

6. What time did you drop off?

7. It is important to grow up.

8. Those kids hang around all day.

9. Keep out!

10. We passed the exam; we lucked out.

5I.

1. My sister is going to break up with her boyfriend tonight.

2. I don't understand how she puts up with her new roommate.

3. He is looking for another teacher to fill in for him tomorrow.

4. The doctor told her to cut back on coffee.

5. If you have a cold, you should keep away from/stay away from other people as much as possible.

6. It is hard for the smaller children to keep up with the big ones.

7. We have to go to the store; we have run out of milk for the baby.

8. The children are worn out from playing all day.

9. They will have to face up to the facts.

10. We all look up to our boss.

5J.

1. blowout
2. hang-ups
3. getaway
4. makeup
5. rip-off
6. show-off
7. tryouts
8. hangout
9. workout
10. write-up

5K.

1. check-out
2. carry-out/take-out
3. wake-up
4. run-down
5. drive-through

6A.

1. downswing
2. upsurge
3. input
4. update
5. outbreak

6B.

1. overjoyed
2. on-line
3. overworked, underpaid
4. outgoing
5. up, down

6C.

1. downgrade
2. overcome
3. withdraw
4. overwhelm
5. outlaw

an	absence	of	40.10	be	affectionate	toward	53.2
be	abhorrent	to	52.5	in the	affirmative		31.25
in one's	absence		31.15	to	affix	to	52.8
to	abuse someone	(all) through	50.7	in the	afternoon		31.3
from one's	accent		30.11	(all) through the	afternoon		50.7
be	acceptable	to	52.5	on nice	afternoons		42.14
in	acceptance		31.30	at one's	age		11.9
be	accessible	for	29.6	under	age		55.3
in	accord	with	59.11	with	age		59.13
on	account	of	40.14	one's	age is	against	5.5
on	account	of	42.19	through an	agency		50.8
in	accounting		31.17	be	aghast	at	11.7
be	accustomed	to	52.6	to	agree	about	1.1
an	ache	in one's ___	31.23	to	agree	on	42.33
be	aching	with	59.18	to	agree	to	52.6
to	act	against	5.3	to	agree	with	59.11
to	act	as	10.1	in	agreement	with	31.22
to	act	for someone	29.9	an	agreement	with	59.11
to	act	like	37.2	in	agreement	with	59.11
to	act	up	58.10	toward an	agreement		53.3
against an	action		5.3	be	ahead	of	6.3
in	action		31.30	in	aid	of	31.20
go into	action		36.4	to one's	aid		52.4
in one's	actions		31.3	to	aim	at	11.3
to	adapt	to	52.6	have an	air	about	1.8
to	add	on	42.32	in the	air		31.35
to	add	to	52.8	on the	air		42.28
to	add	up (to)	58.10	with an	air		59.5
to	add something	on (to)	42.32	in the	air force		31.17
in	addition	to	31.35	by	air mail		22.3
in	addition		31.32	an	airplane	to	52.2
to	adhere	to	52.8	on an	airplane		42.9
be	adjacent	to	52.19	in an	airplane (small)		31.1
in	administration		31.17	off	alcohol		41.4
under an	administration		55.4	in an	alcove		31.1
to	admit	to	52.6	in	alignment	with	31.22
something/nothing	adorable	about	1.5	in	alignment		31.18
be beneath	adultery		16.3		all	along	7.3
in	adulthood		31.3		all	of	40.5
to	advance	in	31.34	after	all		4.8
in	advance		31.3	in	all		31.32
at an	advantage		11.11	be	allergic	to	52.6
	advice	for	29.1	an	allergy	to	52.6
on the	advice	of	42.19	of	aluminum		40.7
to	advise	about	1.1	be	amazed	at	11.7
to	advise someone	of	40.8	in	analysis		31.32
be	affectionate	to	52.7	of	anger		40.6

NOTE: Numbers refer to preposition number and section in Part One.

with	anger		59.5
with	anger		59.18
be at an	angle	to	52.19
from an	angle		30.8
be	angry	about	1.2
in	anguish		31.14
in	anguish	of	40.12
of	anguish		40.6
an	animal	of	40.1
out of	animosity		46.11
for one's	anniversary		29.8
on one's	anniversary		42.25
an	annoyance	to	52.5
to the	annoyance	of	40.12
be	annoying	to	52.5
	another	of	40.5
an	answer	for	29.1
an	answer	to	52.2
an	answer	to	52.6
in	answer	to	31.32
the	answer	to	52.13
the	antidote	to	52.13
out of	anxiety		46.11
be	anxious	about	1.2
be	anxious	for	29.3
	any	of	40.5
like	anything		37.3
at an	apartment		11.1
an	appeal	to	52.6
to	apply	for	29.3
to	apply	to	52.8
in	appreciation	of	31.20
be	appreciative	to	52.7
in	apprenhension		31.25
in	approbation		31.25
in	approval		31.25
on	approval		42.28
on	approval		42.31
an	aptitude	for	29.19
in	architecture		31.17
within an	area		60.1
to	argue	about	1.1
to	argue	against	5.3
to	argue	among	8.2
to	argue	over	48.10
to	argue	with	59.10
an	argument	about	1.1
in an	argument	with	31.22
have an	argument	with	59.10
toward an	argument		53.3

arm-in-	arm	with	31.15
at	arm's length		11.9
be up in	arms	about	58.8
in the	army		31.17
to	arrange	above	2.1
to	arrange	into	36.3
on one's	arrival		42.25
with the	arrival	of	59.18
an	article	about	1.1
an	article	on	42.21
in an	article		31.1
be	ashamed	of	40.13
to	ask	about	1.1
to	ask	for	29.3
to	ask someone	out	46.13
an	assault	on	42.27
in	assent		31.25
to	assist	in	31.34
the	assistant	to	52.15
in an	association		31.2
on the	assumption	of	42.19
	assurance	about	1.1
be	astonished	at	11.7
to one's	astonishment		52.5
be	astounded	at	11.7
to	attach	to	52.8
to	attach something	with	59.8
be	attached	to	52.14
an	attack	on	42.27
pay	attention	to	52.6
at	attention		11.6
be	attentive	to	52.7
in an	attic		31.1
one's	attitude	toward	53.2
after one's	attitude		4.4
something/nothing	attractive	about	1.5
be	attributable	to	52.14
to	audition	for	29.3
on the	authority	of	42.19
be	available	for	29.6
be	available	to	52.7
above	average		2.2
on	average		42.14
under	average		55.3
an	aversion	to	52.6
to	award	to	52.4
an	award	to	52.4
be	aware	of	40.13
in	awe	of	31.14
be	awkward	with	59.5

on the	back	of	40.3
to	back	down (from)	25.5
to	back	off	41.8
to	back	up	58.10
around	back		9.6
be back to	back		52.19
one's	background is	against	5.5
something/nothing	bad	about	1.5
be	bad	at	11.8
be	bad	for	29.6
	bad	of someone	40.15
in	bad weather		31.7
in	badminton		31.29
a	bag	of	40.4
in a	bag		31.1
by the	bag		22.5
to	bake	for	29.1
against one's	balance		5.8
in a	balcony		31.1
on the	balcony		42.2
a	ban	on	42.22
to	bang	against	5.2
to	bank	on	42.13
in	banking		31.17
in	bankruptcy		31.24
go into	bankruptcy		36.4
by the	barrel		22.5
through a	barricade		50.2
a	barrier	to	52.13
through a	barrier		50.2
in	baseball		31.29
be	based	on	42.13
in a	basement		31.1
be	bashful	about	1.2
be	basking	in	31.34
to	bat something	over	48.4
in a	bathing suit		31.16
to	battle	over	48.10
to	be	about	1.8
to	be	across from	3.3
to	be	after	4.3
to	be	ahead of	6.1
to	be	back from	12.2
to	be	beside	17.1
to	be	for	29.21
to	be	from	30.1
to	be	in back of	12.4
to	be	like	37.1
to	be	off	41.1
to	be	on	42.12
to	be	out of	46.4
to	be	out of	46.6
to	be	over	48.1
to	be	over	48.7
to	be	through with	50.5
to	be	under	55.2
to	be	up	58.2
to	be	up to	58.9
to	be	with	59.1
to	be	with	59.2
to	be	with	59.7
to	be	with	59.11
to	be	with	59.14
to	be	with	59.20
off the	beach		41.3
on the	beach		42.2
on the	beach		42.7
be	beaming	with	59.18
to	beat	against	5.2
to the	beat	of	52.16
to	beat	to a pulp	52.17
with all one's	beauty		59.18
	because	of	40.14
in	bed		31.1
to	bed		52.1
to	beg	for	29.3
to	beg	off	41.8
to	begin	with	59.12
from the	beginning	of	30.6
from	beginning	to end	30.6
at the	beginning		11.4
from the	beginning		30.2
on	behalf	of	42.19
to	behave	like	37.2
one's	behavior	toward	53.2
after one's	behavior		4.4
on one's best	behavior		42.28
beyond	belief		20.2
be	belligerent	with	59.5
to	belong	to	52.14
below the	belt		15.4
on the	bench		42.28
to	bend	over	48.1
go around the	bend		9.6
be	beneficial	to	52.5
to one's	benefit		52.4
at	best		11.10
be for the	best		29.23
to	bet	on	42.13
be	better	for someone	29.6

be	better	from	30.9
be	better	off	41.7
for	better or	for worse	29.23
in	between		19.8
the great	beyond		20.4
on a	bicycle		42.10
a	bill	for	29.14
against a	bill		5.3
against one's	bill		5.8
in	bills		31.19
with the	bills		59.18
to	bind	to	52.20
through	binoculars		50.8
a	bird	of	40.1
with the	birth	of	59.18
on one's	birth		42.25
for one's	birthday		29.8
on one's	birthday		42.25
quite a	bit	about	1.1
into	bits		36.3
in	black		31.16
in the	black		31.14
in	black and white		31.11
to the	blare	of	52.16
be	blessed	with	59.4
	blind	in	31.33
on the	blink		42.28
around the	block		9.1
to	blow	down	25.3
to	blow something	down	25.3
to	blow	into	36.1
to	blow something	into	36.1
to	blow	off	41.1
to	blow something	off	41.1
to	blow something	out	46.13
to	blow	over	48.14
to	blow	toward	53.1
to	blow	up	58.10
to	blow something	up	58.10
above	board		2.6
across the	board		3.4
go by the	board		22.10
on the	board		42.24
on	board		42.28
on the	boardwalk		42.3
in a	boat (small)		31.1
in	bold		31.11
to	bone	up on	58.10
a	book	about	1.1
a	book	on	42.21

in a	book		31.1
to	book someone	for	29.4
a	boost	to	52.13
to	boot	up	58.10
on the	border	of	42.6
to	bore	to death	52.17
be	bored	from	30.9
be	bored	with	59.6
be	boring	to	52.5
to	borrow	from	30.1
to	borrow something	from	30.1
under a	boss		55.4
	both	of	40.5
to	bother	about	1.1
a	bother	to	52.5
on the	bottom	of	42.6
to	bounce	on	42.8
out of	bounds		46.10
within	bounds		60.4
have a	bout	with	59.10
a	bowl	of	40.4
a	box	of	40.4
in a	box		31.1
by the	box		22.5
through the	boxes		50.6
in	braces		31.16
to	brag	about	1.1
in	braids		31.16
a	brand	of	40.4
of	brass		40.7
to	break	down	25.3
to	break something	down	25.3
to	break	in (on)	31.36
to	break something	in	31.36
to	break	into	36.1
to	break	into	36.3
to	break	into	36.6
to	break	off	41.2
to	break something	off	41.8
to	break	out	46.13
to	break	up	58.10
to	break	up (with)	59.15
to	break something	up	58.10
at	breakfast		11.2
for	breakfast		29.8
over	breakfast		48.9
(all) through	breakfast		50.7
to	breakfast		52.1
above	breaking the law		2.5
beneath	breaking the law		16.3

a	breath	of	40.6
out of	breath		46.6
a	bridge	to	52.2
in the game of	bridge		31.29
in	brief		31.12
to	bring	about	1.9
to	bring	back	12.3
to	bring	back to	12.1
to	bring	down	25.2
to	bring	down	25.3
to	bring something	down	25.3
to	bring	from	30.1
to	bring something	in	31.5
to	bring	on	42.32
to	bring something	through	50.2
to	bring	to	52.3
to	bring something	up	58.1
to	bring something	up	58.10
on the	brink		42.28
to	broadcast something	all over the …	48.8
at a	brunch		11.2
to	brush something	off	41.1
to	brush	up (on)	58.10
by the	bucket		22.5
on a	budget		42.28
be over one's	budget		48.2
to	build	for	29.1
to	build	on	42.32
to	build something	on (to)	42.32
to	build something	out of	46.8
in a	building		31.1
through a	building		50.1
through the	building		50.6
within a	building		60.1
by the	bunch		22.5
in	bunches		31.18
in	bundles		31.18
to	burn	down	25.3
to	burn	up	58.10
to	burn something	up	58.10
to	burst	in	31.5
to	burst	into flames	36.5
to	bury something	under	55.2
a	bus	to	52.2
on a	bus		42.9
at a	bus stop		11.1
by the	bushel		22.5
do	business	with	59.11
in	business	with	31.17

on	business		42.19
in	busloads		31.26
to	butt	against	5.1
to	butt	in	31.5
to	butt	in	31.36
to	buy	for	29.1
to	buy something	for	29.13
to	buy	from	30.1
to	buy something	from	30.1
a good	buy	on	42.22
the	buzz	of	40.6
to the	buzz	of	52.16
by and	by		22.10
in	cahoots	with	31.22
in	cahoots	with	59.11
on the	calculations	of	42.19
to	call	back	12.3
to	call	for	29.3
to	call	from	30.1
to	call	on	42.37
to	call something	off	41.8
to	call someone	up	58.10
on	call		42.28
above the	call of duty		2.6
to	calm someone	down	25.5
on	calories		42.16
to	campaign	against	5.3
to	campaign	for	29.3
a	can	of	40.4
in the game of	canasta		31.29
in a	canoe		31.1
be	capable	of	40.8
in	capital letters		31.11
the	captain	of	40.1
in	captivity		31.24
in a	car		31.1
a	card	to	52.2
of	cardboard		40.7
in a game of	cards		31.29
to	care	about	1.1
to	care	for	29.24
under the	care	of	55.4
with	care		59.5
to	care for someone	(all) through	50.7
be	careless	of	40.15
through	carelessness		50.9
in	carloads		31.26
to	carry	above	2.1
to	carry	back to	12.1
to	carry	down	25.2

to	carry	on (with)	42.37
to	carry something	out	46.1
to	carry something	over	48.4
to	carry	through with	50.10
to	carry something	through	50.2
to	carry something	through	50.10
to	carry	to	52.3
to	carry	to extremes	52.17
to	carry	to the limits	52.17
to	carry something	up	58.1
to	carve something	out of	46.8
in	case	of	31.32
the	case	to	52.15
in any	case		31.32
in that	case		31.32
in one's	case		31.32
in	cash		31.19
at the	cash register		11.5
on	cassette		42.15
to	catch	on (to)	42.37
to	catch	up on	58.10
to	catch	up (with)	58.10
the	category	of	40.4
in a	category		31.2
be	caught	with	59.4
be	caused	by	22.1
on the	ceiling		42.4
to	celebrate	among	8.2
to	celebrate	with	59.12
in	celebration	of	31.20
at a	celebration		11.2
of	celebration		40.9
to	center	on	42.34
in	centimeters		31.21
in a	century		31.3
without	ceremony		61.5
be	certain	of	40.13
to one's	chagrin		52.5
in a	chair		31.1
a	challenge	for	29.8
the	challenge	of	40.12
a	challenge	to	52.5
be	challenging	for	29.6
by	chance		22.10
by (any)	chance		22.10
off	chance		41.7
a	change	in	31.34
a	change	of pace	40.11
a	change	of scenery	40.11
for a	change		29.23

in	change		31.19
with the	change		59.18
in	chaos		31.14
on the	charge	of	42.19
in	charge		31.24
be	charged	with	59.20
against one's	charges		5.8
be	charitable	toward	53.2
with all one's	charm		59.18
be	charming	about	1.1
be	charming	to	52.7
off the	charts		41.7
to	chase something	from	30.2
to	chat	with	59.1
to	cheat	(all) through	50.7
to	cheat	on	42.35
above	cheating		2.5
be beneath	cheating		16.3
a	check	for	29.14
to	check	in	31.36
to	check something	in	31.36
to	check	into	36.6
to	check something	off	41.8
to	check	out	46.13
to	check something	out	46.13
to	check	out (of)	46.13
in	check		31.24
in	checks		31.19
tongue in	cheek		31.12
to	cheer	at	11.7
to	cheer	for	29.21
to	cheer	up	58.10
to	cheer someone	up	58.10
in the game of	chess		31.29
to	chew someone	out	46.13
to	chicken	out (on)	46.13
to	chide someone	for	29.4
in	childhood		31.3
to	chill	to the bone	52.17
to	chip	in	31.36
in a	choir		31.2
to	choke	on	42.18
to	choose	as	10.1
to	choose	between	19.3
to	chop	off	41.2
to	chop	up	58.8
in a	chorus		31.2
in	chorus		31.12
at	church		11.2
in	church		31.1

to	church		52.1
off	cigarettes		41.4
in a	circle		31.18
in	circulation		31.24
under the	circumstances		55.5
to	cite someone	for	29.4
a	citizen	of	40.1
the	city	of	40.2
of a	city		40.1
in a	city		31.1
all over the	city		48.8
through the	city		50.1
all through the	city		50.6
within a	city		60.1
to	clash	with	59.10
to	clash	with	59.16
a	class	of	40.4
at a	class		11.2
in	class		31.1
of	clay		40.7
to	clean something	off	41.1
to	clean	up	58.9
to	clean something	up	58.10
to	clean	with	59.8
to	clean something	with	59.8
to	clear something	off	41.1
to	clear something	with	59.8
to	climb	on	42.8
to	climb	over	48.4
a	climb	to	52.2
to	climb	up	58.1
to	cling	on	42.12
be	close	up	58.9
be	close	to	52.19
to	close	down	25.5
to	close something	down	25.5
to	close	in (on)	31.36
to	close	out (of)	46.13
to	close	up	58.10
to	close something	up	58.10
to	close	with	59.12
through the	closets		50.6
through the	clouds		50.3
of a	club		40.1
in a	club		31.2
a	clue	to	52.13
under a	coach		55.4
off the	coast		41.3
in the	coast guard		31.17
in a	coat		31.16

in a	cocoon		31.1
in	code		31.12
over	coffee		48.9
in	coins		31.19
be	cold	to	52.7
in the	cold		31.7
in	cold blood		31.15
in	cold weather		31.7
to	collaborate	with	59.11
in	collaboration	with	31.22
in	collaboration	with	59.11
to	collect	from	30.1
to	collect something	from	30.2
in	collusion	with	31.22
the	color	of	40.4
the	color	of	40.6
to	color	with	59.8
in	color		31.11
in a	color		31.16
off	color		41.7
in	combination	with	31.22
to	come	about	1.9
to	come	across	3.5
to	come	after	4.3
to	come	back from	12.2
to	come	down	25.1
to	come	down	25.2
to	come	down with	25.5
to	come	from	30.1
to	come	in	31.5
to	come	into	36.1
to	come	off	41.1
to	come	out of	46.3
to	come	through	50.10
to	come	to	52.1
to	come	to	52.22
to	come	up with	58.9
in	comfort		31.14
be	comfortable	with	59.6
on	command		42.19
in	commemoration	of	31.20
to	comment	about	1.1
out of	commission		46.7
be	committed	to	52.14
on a	committee		42.24
be beneath	committing a crime		16.3
in	common	with	31.22
on	compact disc		42.15
of a	company	of	40.1
be	comparable	to	52.12

be	comparable	with	59.17
to	compare	to	52.12
to	compare	with	59.16
to	compare something	with	59.16
	compared	to	52.12
in	comparison	with	31.22
in	comparison		31.30
out of	compassion		46.11
with	compassion		59.5
to	compensate someone	for	29.4
in	compensation	for	31.20
to	compete	for	29.3
to	compete	with	59.10
in	competition	with	31.22
be in	competition	with	59.10
to	complain	about	1.1
to	complain	of	40.8
a	complaint	about	1.1
about	complete		1.7
in	compliance	with	59.11
in	compliance		31.25
to	comply	with	59.11
be	composed	of	40.7
beyond	comprehension		20.2
be	comprised	of	40.7
at the	computer		11.5
on the	computer		42.16
on the	computer		42.17
in	computers		31.17
to	concentrate	on	42.34
against a	concept		5.3
be	concerned	about	1.2
be	concerned	with	59.7
in	concert	with	59.11
at a	concert		11.2
in	concert		31.12
in	conclusion		31.30
in	conclusion		31.32
toward a	conclusion		53.3
to	concur	with	59.11
in	concurrence	with	59.11
in	condition		31.14
get into	condition		36.4
on	condition		42.28
under the	conditions		55.5
to	conduct	for someone	29.9
one's	conduct	toward	53.2
at a	conference		11.2
in	confidence		31.15
to	confine	to	52.20
in	confinement		31.24
in	conflict	with	31.22
to	conflict	with	59.10
be in	conflict	with	59.10
in	conflict		31.24
be	confused	about	1.2
be	confusing	to	52.5
in	confusion		31.14
in	confusion		31.25
to	congratulate someone	for	29.4
	congratulations	on	42.25
in	conjunction	with	31.22
be	connected	to	52.14
in	connection	with	31.22
be	conscientious	of	40.15
be	conscious	of	40.13
to	consent	to	52.6
in	consent		31.25
be	considerate	to	52.7
be	considerate	toward	53.2
under	consideration		55.5
under	construction		55.5
to	contact	about	1.1
in	contact	with	31.22
through a	contact		50.8
a	container	of	40.4
in	contempt		31.25
be	content	with	59.6
have a	contest	with	59.10
out of	context		46.7
in a	continent		31.1
a	contract	with	59.11
under a	contract		55.4
on the	contrary		42.36
to	contrast	with	59.16
in	contrast		31.30
to	contribute something	toward	53.4
under the	control	of	55.4
have	control	over	48.6
in	control		31.24
out of	control		46.7
under	control		55.4
a	conversation	about	1.1
in	conversation		31.30
to	converse	with	59.1
to	cook	for	29.1
to	cook	to perfection	52.17

be	cool	toward	53.2	to	crawl	out of	46.3
to	cooperate	in	31.34	be	crazy	about	1.2
to	cooperate	with	59.11	be	crazy	of someone	40.15
in	cooperation	with	31.22	like	crazy		37.3
in	cooperation	with	59.11	to	create	for	29.1
the	coordinator	of	40.1	to	create something	out of	46.8
of	copper		40.7	be	created	from	30.7
to	copy	from	30.1	a	credit	to	52.5
be	cordial	to	52.7	on	credit		42.16
in a	corner		31.1	be up a	creek		58.8
in a	corner		31.24	to	creep	up	58.1
on the	corner		42.2	on the	crew		42.24
through the	correspondence		50.6	with the	crime		59.18
the	cost	of	40.4	to	criticize someone	for	29.4
in	costume		31.16	to	cross	over	48.4
of	cotton		40.7	to	cross something	out	46.1
on the	council		42.24	be	crucial	for	29.6
to	count	on	42.13	be	crucial	to	52.5
to	count	up to	58.9	be	crude	of someone	40.15
to	count someone	in	31.36	be	cruel	of someone	40.15
at a	counter		11.1	be	cruel	to	52.7
of a	country		40.1	above	cruelty		2.5
across the	country		3.4	out of	cruelty		46.11
in a	country		31.1	a	cruise	to	52.2
all over the	country		48.8	to	cruise	up	58.5
through the	country		50.1	to	cruise	with	59.14
all through the	country		50.6	on a	cruise		42.20
within a	country		60.1	to	crush	against	5.2
within a	county		60.1	have a	crush	on	42.33
a	couple	of	40.5	to	cry	(all) through	50.7
with	courage		59.5	to	cry	about	1.1
off	course		41.4	to	cry	for	29.3
on	course		42.28	to	cry	in	31.25
through (with) a	course		50.5	the	cry	of	40.6
on the	court		42.3	a	cry	of	40.6
the	cover	to	52.15	to	cry	over	48.10
to	cover something	with	59.9	with a	cry		59.5
be	covered	in	31.34	be	crying	with	59.18
to	crack	down (on)	25.5	of	crystal		40.7
to	craft something	out of	46.8	of a	culture		40.1
be	crafted	from	30.7	by the	cup		22.5
to	cram	into	36.1	a	cure	for	29.1
to	cram something	with	59.9	a	cure	for	29.3
to	crash	against	5.2	be	cured	of	40.11
to	crash	into	36.2	out of	curiosity		46.11
the	crash	of	40.6	in	curls		31.16
to	crawl	about	1.6	against the	current		5.4
to	crawl	across	3.1	with the	current		59.14
to	crawl	all over the …	48.8	be	curt	with	59.5
to	crawl	back to	12.1	through the	curtains		50.2

be	customary	for someone	29.6
through	customs		50.2
to	cut	back (on)	12.5
to	cut	down	25.3
to	cut something	down	25.3
to	cut	in/into	31.8
to	cut	into	36.3
to	cut	off	41.2
to	cut something	out	46.1
to	cut	with	59.8
to	cut something	with	59.8
to	cut ties	with	59.15
something/nothing	cute	about	1.5
to	dance	for	29.1
to	dance	with	59.1
at a	dance		11.2
to	dance something	with	59.1
be	dancing	with	59.18
in	danger		31.14
get into	danger		36.4
out of	danger		46.10
in the	dark		31.24
out of	date		46.7
be up to	date		58.8
towards	dawn		54.1
a	day	of	40.9
day after	day		4.7
by	day		22.10
by the	day		22.4
(all) through the	day		50.7
over the next few	days		48.9
a	dearth	of	40.10
with the	death	of	59.18
in	death		31.3
on one's	death		42.25
a	debate	against	5.3
a	debate	among	8.2
a	debate	on	42.21
in	debate	with	31.22
in a	debate	with	31.22
at a	debate		11.2
against one's	debt		5.8
in	debt		31.24
go into	debt		36.4
in a	decade		31.3
of the	decade		40.1
to	decide	between	19.3
a	decline	in	31.34
a	decrease	in	31.34
with the	decrease	in	59.18
to	dedicate something	to	52.4
to	dedicate something	with	59.12
be	dedicated	to	52.14
in	dedication	of	31.20
a	dedication	to	52.4
in one's	deeds		31.3
in	defeat		31.25
in	defeat		31.3
in	deference	to	31.15
in	defiance		31.25
to	delete something	from	30.3
to the	delight	of	52.5
in	delight		31.25
of	delight		40.6
to one's	delight		52.5
with	delight		59.5
be	delighted	for someone	29.7
be	delighted	with	59.6
be	delightful	of someone	40.15
to	deliver	to	52.3
in	demand		31.24
on	demand		42.31
one's	demeanor	toward	53.2
with the	departure	of	59.18
on one's	departure		42.25
to	depend	on	42.13
to	depend	on	42.36
be	dependent	on	42.13
go into a	depression		36.4
a	depth	of	40.4
to	derive	from	30.1
of a	descent		40.1
to	describe	to	52.3
to	design	for	29.1
a	desire	of	40.12
at a	desk		11.1
in	desolation		31.25
in	despair		31.14
in	detail		31.12
through	determination		50.9
a	detriment	to	52.5
be	detrimental	to	52.5
be	developed	from	30.7
to	devote	to	52.4
be	devoted	to	52.7
on the	diamond (baseball)		42.3
the	dictator	of	40.1
under a	dictator		55.4
under the	dictatorship	of	55.4
in a	dictionary		31.1

to	die	of	40.11
to	die	on someone	42.35
off one's	diet		41.4
on a	diet		42.28
to	differ	from	30.4
to	differ	with	59.10
be	different	from	30.3
to	dig	with	59.8
to	dig something	with	59.8
of	dignity		40.16
in	dimes		31.19
at	dinner		11.2
for	dinner		29.8
over	dinner		48.9
(all) through	dinner		50.7
to	dinner		52.1
towards	dinnertime		54.1
in	dire straits		31.14
to	direct	for someone	29.9
to	direct someone	toward	53.1
under the	direction	of	55.4
in this/that	direction		31.9
the	directions	for	29.3
the	directions	to	52.13
at a	disadvantage		11.11
to	disagree	with	59.10
a	disagreement	about	1.1
have a	disagreement	with	59.10
be	disappointed	with	59.6
in	disappointment		31.25
to one's	disappointment		52.5
in	disarray		31.14
in	disaster		31.14
to one's	discomfort		52.5
a	discount	on	42.22
at a	discount		11.9
a	discredit	to	52.5
at one's	discretion		11.11
with	discretion		59.5
to	discuss something	among	8.2
a	discussion	about	1.1
a	discussion	on	42.21
in a	discussion	with	59.1
under	discussion		55.5
in	disdain		31.25
with	disdain		59.5
in	disgrace		31.14
in	disgrace		31.25
to one's	disgrace		52.5
in	disguise		31.16

in	disgust		31.25
to one's	disgust		52.5
to the	disgust	of	40.12
above	dishonesty		2.5
on	disk		42.15
in	dismay		31.25
in	disobedience		31.25
in	disorder		31.14
on	display		42.28
by	disposition		22.10
in	dispute	with	31.22
be	disrespectful	of	40.13
in	dissent		31.25
to	dissociate something	from	30.3
at a	distance		11.9
be	distasteful	to	52.5
to	distinguish something	from	30.4
with	distress		59.5
to	distribute	among	8.3
to	distribute	to	52.3
a	distrust	of	40.12
a	disturbance	to	52.5
be	disturbing	to	52.5
to	dive	off	41.1
to	divide	in/into	31.8
to	divide	into	36.3
to	divide	up	58.9
to	do	about	1.1
to	do	for	29.1
to	do someone	in	31.36
to	do something	for	29.13
to	do something	over	48.11
to	do well	by someone	22.11
under a	doctor		55.4
in	dollars		31.19
to	donate	to	52.3
to	donate something	toward	53.4
a	donation	to	52.2
be	done	by	22.1
about	done		1.7
the	door	to	52.15
through a	door		50.2
door to	door		52.11
out of	doors		46.12
to	dote	on	42.34
in	doubt		31.14
without a	doubt		61.5
	down	with	59.20

by the	dozen		22.5
by the	dozens		22.8
to	drag	around	9.9
to	drag	on	42.26
in	drag		31.16
to	drag something	up	58.1
to	drape something	on	42.12
to	drape something	over	48.5
to	draw	around	9.3
to	draw something	in	31.5
to	draw	up	58.7
to	draw	with	59.8
to	draw something	with	59.8
in a	drawer		31.1
through the	drawers		50.6
in	dread		31.14
be	dreadful	to	52.7
to	dream	about	1.1
to	dream	of	40.8
to	dream	up	58.7
in one's	dreams		31.3
to	dress	up	58.9
in a	dress		31.16
to	drift	with	59.14
to	drink	out of	46.3
to	drink	with	59.1
to	drink something	with	59.1
over	drinks		48.9
to	drip something	on	42.8
to	drip	onto	43.1
to	drip something	onto	43.1
to	drive	across	3.1
to	drive	against	5.4
to	drive	all over the ...	48.8
to	drive	around	9.1
to	drive	around	9.8
to	drive	back from	12.2
to	drive	back to	12.1
to	drive	down	25.2
to	drive	for someone	29.9
to	drive	from	30.1
to	drive	away from	30.3
to	drive	into	36.1
to	drive something	into	36.1
to	drive	off	41.1
to	drive something	off	41.1
to	drive	on	42.26
to	drive	out of	46.3
to	drive something	out of	46.3
to	drive	over	48.4

to	drive something	over	48.4
to	drive	to	52.1
to	drive	to distraction	52.17
to	drive	to insanity	52.17
to	drive	up	58.5
to	drive	with	59.14
go for a	drive		29.23
in	drive		31.24
to	drop	by	22.11
to	drop	in	31.36
to	drop	in (on)	31.36
to	drop	off	41.8
to	drop	out of	46.13
by the	drop		22.5
to	drop something	by	22.11
to	drop something	in	31.1
to	drop something	in	31.5
to	drop something	on	42.8
to	drop something	onto	43.1
be	drowning	in	31.34
off	drugs		41.4
to	drum	up	58.6
be	drunk	from	30.9
to	dry something	with	59.8
in	duplicate		31.11
towards	dusk		54.1
off	duty		41.4
on	duty		42.28
to	dwell	on	42.34
to	dwell	over	48.7
	each	of	40.5
be	eager	for	29.3
an	ear	for	29.19
at the	earliest		11.10
in	earnest		31.15
be up to one's	ears	in	58.8
on	earth		42.3
at	ease		11.6
be	easy	on	42.34
to	eat	out	46.13
to	eat	out of	46.3
to	eat	with	59.1
to	eat	with	59.8
to	eat something	with	59.1
to	eat something	with	59.8
on the	edge	of	42.6
on	edge		42.28
on the	edge		42.28
for all one's	education		29.17
with all one's	education		59.18

	either	of	40.5
in the	eighties		31.3
of	elation		40.6
to	elect	as	10.1
on	electricity		42.16
to	eliminate something	from	30.3
an	embargo	on	42.22
to one's	embarrassment		52.5
to	empathize	with	59.11
an	encumbrance	on	42.22
in an	encyclopedia		31.1
on the	end	of	42.6
to	end	with	59.12
at the	end		11.4
in the	end		31.30
toward an	ending		53.3
against an	enemy		5.3
get up (enough)	energy		58.6
be	engaged	to	52.14
in	English		31.12
the	enjoyment	of	40.12
	enough	of	40.5
in	entertainment		31.17
with	enthusiasm		59.5
through an	entrance		50.2
be	envious	of	40.13
to	erase something	from	30.3
to	erase something	with	59.8
to	err	on	42.34
through an	error		50.9
the	essays	of	40.1
be	even	with	59.17
in the	evening		31.3
towards	evening		54.1
on nice	evenings		42.14
	evidence	on	42.22
the	evil	of	40.15
through (with)	exams		50.5
be	excellent	at	11.8
in an	exchange	with	31.22
to	exchange something	for	29.13
be	excited	about	1.2
the	excitement	of	40.12
of	excitement		40.6
to	exclaim	in	31.25
be	exclusive	to	52.14
on an	excursion		42.20
for	exercise		29.5
of	exercise		40.9
be	exhausted	from	30.9
something/nothing	exotic	about	1.5
to	expel someone	for	29.4
to	expel someone	from	30.2
for all one's	experience		29.17
with	experience		59.13
for all one's	expertise		29.17
to	explain	to	52.3
an	explanation	to	52.2
to	expound	on	42.21
with an	expression		59.5
to	extend	to	52.1
on the	exterior	of	42.6
an	eye	for	29.19
under the	eye	of	55.4
in the	eye		31.23
of	fabric		40.7
through the	fabric		50.3
to	fabricate something	out of	46.8
be face to	face	(with)	52.19
about	face	about	1.8
to	face	up to	58.10
in	fact		31.32
at a	factory		11.1
on the	faculty		42.24
without	fail		61.5
after one's	failure		4.4
to	faint	on someone	42.35
in	fairness		31.15
of a	faith		40.1
of	faith		40.16
be	faithful	to	52.7
to	fall	down	25.1
to	fall	for	29.24
to	fall	into	36.1
to	fall	off	41.1
to	fall	on	42.8
to	fall	on	42.18
to	fall	onto	43.1
to	fall	out (of)	46.3
to	fall	out (with)	59.15
to	fall	over	48.14
to	fall	through	50.10
to	fall	to	52.1
to	fall asleep	on	42.35
something/nothing	familiar	about	1.5
of a	family		40.1
in a	family		31.2

keep within the	family		60.5
be	famous	for	29.4
by	far		22.9
something/nothing	fascinating	about	1.5
be	fascinating	to	52.5
in	fashion		31.13
out of	fashion		46.7
to	fashion something	out of	46.8
be	fashioned	from	30.7
to	fasten	around	9.3
to	fasten	with	59.8
be	fat	from	30.9
through the	fault	of	50.9
with all one's	faults		59.19
a	favor	to	52.4
at the	fax machine		11.5
for	fear	of	29.23
a	fear	of	40.12
in	fear		31.14
of	fear		40.6
out of	fear		46.11
with	fear		59.5
with	fear		59.18
be	feared	for	29.4
the	feel	of	40.4
the	feel	of	40.6
to	feel	up to	58.10
with	feeling		59.5
one's	feelings	toward	53.2
in	feet		31.21
on the	fence		42.2
on the	fence		42.28
of	festivity		40.9
	few	of	40.5
a	few	of	40.5
in a	few words		31.12
on the	field		42.2
on the	field		42.3
all over the	field		48.8
on a	field trip		42.20
in the	fifties		31.3
in	fifties		31.19
to	fight	against	5.3
to	fight	against	5.4
to	fight	among	8.2
to	fight	for	29.3
to	fight	over	48.10
in a	fight	with	31.22
to	fight	with	59.10
to	figure something	out	46.13
in a	file		31.1
through the	files		50.6
to	fill	in (for)	31.36
to	fill in	for someone	29.9
to	fill something	in	31.36
to	fill something	out	46.13
to	fill something	up	58.10
to	fill something	with	59.9
on	film		42.15
in the	final analysis		31.32
to	find	out (about)	1.1
to	find something	out	46.13
to	find something	under	55.2
to	find something	under	55.6
to	fine someone	for	29.4
be	finished	with	59.15
about	finished		1.7
on	fire		42.28
at	first		11.4
something/nothing	fishy	about	1.5
in	fives		31.19
be	flexible	with	59.5
a	flight	to	52.2
on a	flight		42.20
to	flirt	around	9.8
to	float	over	48.1
to	float	with	59.14
to	float something	over	48.1
on the	floor		42.4
all over the	floor		48.8
against the	flow		5.4
with the	flow		59.14
to	fly	around	9.1
to	fly	back from	12.2
to	fly	back to	12.1
to	fly	from	30.1
to	fly something	in	31.5
to	fly	into	36.1
to	fly	over	48.1
to	fly something	over	48.1
to	fly	to	52.1
to	fly	toward	53.1
out of	focus		46.7
in the	fog		31.7
through the	fog		50.3
in	foggy weather		31.7
in a	folder		31.1
in	folds		31.18
to	follow something	through	50.10
be	fond	of	40.13

on	food		42.16		at a	game		11.2
to	fool	around (with)	9.9		off one's	game		41.4
on	foot		42.10		(all) through the	game		50.7
in the game of	football		31.29		all through the	garden		50.6
against a	force		5.3		on	gas		42.16
against the	force		5.4		out of	gas		46.6
to	force something	on	42.32		through a	gate		50.2
to	force something	through	50.2		to	gaze	into	36.1
be beneath	forgery		16.3		in	gear		31.24
to	forget	about	1.1		of a	gender		40.1
a	form	of	40.4		in	general		31.32
be	formed	of	40.7		under a	general		55.4
be	forthcoming	with	59.5		through the	generosity	of	50.9
at a	forum		11.2		be	generous	with	59.5
be	found	with	59.4		of a	genus		40.1
on all	fours		42.10		to	get	about	1.9
be	frank	with	59.5		to	get something	across to	3.5
in a	fraternity		31.2		to	get something	across (to)	5.4
for	free		29.13		to	get	ahead (of)	6.4
down a	freeway		25.2		to	get	along with	7.4
to	freeze	to death	52.17		to	get	along with	59.11
through a	friend		50.8		to	get	around	9.11
be	friendly	to	52.7		to	get	around to	9.11
be	friendly	toward	53.2		to	get	back	12.5
be	friendly	with	59.5		to	get someone	back	12.5
a	friendship	with	59.11		to	get something back	to/from	12.3
in	friendship		31.15					
from	front	to back	30.5		to	get	back at	12.5
to	frost something	with	59.9		to	get	back from	12.2
to	frown	at	11.3		to	get	back to	12.5
with a	frown		59.5		to	get	by	22.11
be	frustrated	with	59.6		to	get someone	for	29.4
the	frustration	of	40.12		to	get something	for	29.1
of	frustration		40.6		to	get something	from	30.1
through	frustration		50.9		to	get	in	31.5
on	fuel		42.16		to	get	in	31.36
in	full		31.12		to	get something	in	31.1
be	fuming	with	59.18		to	get something	in	31.36
for	fun		29.5		to	get	into	36.1
in	fun		31.15		to	get something	into	36.1
like	fun		37.3		to	get	off	41.1
of	fun		40.9		to	get	off	41.8
at a	function		11.2		to	get something	off	41.1
at a	funeral		11.2		to	get something	off	41.5
through a	funnel		50.1		to	get something	off	41.8
something/nothing	funny	about	1.5		to	get	on	42.8
be	furnished	with	59.4		to	get	on	42.9
in the	future		31.3		to	get	on	42.37
to	gain weight	on	42.16		to	get something	on	42.11
by the	gallon		22.5		to	get something	on	42.37

to	get	on with	59.21
to	get something	out	46.1
to	get	out of	46.3
to	get	out (of)	46.13
to	get something	out (of)	46.3
to	get	over	48.4
to	get	through (with)	50.5
to	get	to	52.1
to	get	up	58.9
to	get something	up	58.10
to	get away	from	30.3
to	get away	with	59.21
to	get sick	on	42.35
be	getting	at	11.11
a	gift	for	29.1
a	gift	to	52.2
a	gift	to	52.4
to	give	in	31.36
to	give	up (on)	58.10
to	give something	back (to/from)	12.3
to	give something	out	46.2
to	give something	to	52.3
to	give something	to	52.4
to	give something	toward	53.4
to	give something	up	58.10
be	glad	about	1.2
to	glare	at	11.3
of	glass		40.7
through the	glass		50.3
through	glasses		50.8
with	glee		59.5
with	glee		59.18
to	glue something	on	42.5
to	glue something	to	52.8
be	glued	to	52.8
to	go	about	1.6
to	go	across	3.1
to	go	after	4.3
to	go	against	5.3
to	go	against	5.4
to	go	around (with)	9.8
to	go	back to	12.1
to	go	by	22.11
to	go	down	25.1
to	go	down	25.2
to	go	for	29.3
to	go	for	29.24
to	go	in	31.5
to	go	in for	29.24
to	go	into	36.1
to	go	off	41.1
to	go	on	42.9
to	go	on	42.26
to	go	out for	29.4
to	go	out (of)	46.3
to	go	out with	46.13
to	go	over	48.4
to	go	through	50.6
to	go	through (with)	50.5
to	go	to	52.1
to	go	toward	53.1
to	go	toward	53.4
to	go	up	58.1
to	go	up	58.5
to	go	with	59.1
to	go	with	59.14
to	go	with	59.16
to	go	ahead	6.2
to	go away	in	31.25
to	go out	for	29.3
to	go quiet	on	42.35
toward a	goal		53.3
of	gold		40.7
in the game of	golf		31.29
something/nothing	good	about	1.5
be	good	at	11.8
be	good	for someone	29.6
be	good	of	40.15
in	good	with	31.22
for	good		29.15
be	good enough	for someone	29.6
in	good hands	with	31.24
in	good weather		31.7
to	goof	around	9.9
to	goof	off	41.8
to	gossip	about	1.1
through	gossip		50.8
above	gossiping		2.5
be beneath	gossiping		16.3
in	government		31.17
to	grab	at	11.3
to	grab something	out of	46.3
up for	grabs		29.10
with	grace		59.5
be	gracious	to	52.7
be	gracious	toward	53.2
to	graduate	from	30.1
a	graduate	of	40.1
for one's	graduation		29.8
against the	grain		5.9

through the	grapevine		50.8
be	grateful	for	29.6
be	grateful	to	52.6
be	gratifying	to	52.5
with	gratitude		59.5
be	great	at	11.8
through	greed		50.9
be	greedy	for	29.3
with a	greeting		59.5
in	grief		31.25
to	grieve	over	48.10
to	grin	at	11.3
to	grind	to a pulp	52.17
to	grind	to dust	52.17
to	groan	about	1.1
a	groan	of	40.6
on the	ground		42.2
on solid	ground		42.3
a	group	of	40.8
of a	group		40.1
in a	group		31.2
in a	group		31.18
in	groups		31.18
in	groups	of a number	31.26
to	grow	up	58.10
to	growl	at	11.3
the	growl	of	40.6
to	grumble	at	11.7
with a	grumble		59.5
with a	grunt		59.5
to	guard	against	5.7
on	guard		42.28
to	guess	at	11.7
with the	guests		59.18
a	guide	to	52.13
to	guide someone	toward	53.1
the	gush	of	40.6
to	gush	over	48.10
in a	hall		31.1
in/into	halves		31.8
to	hand something	in (to)	31.5
to	hand something	out (to)	46.2
to	hand something	out among	8.3
to	hand something	over (to)	48.14
to	hand over something	for	29.13
to	hand something	to	52.3
hand-in-	hand		31.15
off	hand		41.7
on	hand		42.28
on the other	hand		42.36
with a	handshake		59.5
lay	hands	on	42.34
on one's	hands and knees		42.10
to	hang	above	2.1
to	hang	against	5.1
to	hang	around	9.9
to	hang	around with	9.11
to	hang	on	42.12
to	hang something	on	42.12
to	hang	out with	46.13
to	hang	over	48.1
to	hang something	over	48.1
to	hang something	over	48.5
to	hang	up (on)	58.10
to	hang something	up	58.10
to	hang one's head	in	31.25
the	happiness	of	40.12
for	happiness		29.5
in	happiness		31.25
of	happiness		40.6
of	happiness		40.9
with	happiness		59.5
with	happiness		59.18
be	happy	about	1.2
be	happy	for someone	29.7
be	happy	with	59.6
to	harass	about	1.1
be	hard	on	42.34
from	hard work		30.8
to	hark	back to	12.1
be	harmful	to	52.5
to	harmonize	with	59.11
in	harmony		31.12
in	harmony	with	31.22
in	harmony	with	59.11
to	harp	on	42.34
in a	hat		31.16
be	hateful	of	40.15
the	hatred	of	40.12
with	hatred		59.5
to	have it	out with	59.10
to	have something	on	42.11
to	have something	over	48.5
to	have something	over	48.14
to	head	for	29.11
the	head	of	40.1
be	head	over heels	48.12
to	head	toward	53.1
to	head	toward	53.3

be over one's	head		48.2
in (the field of)	health		31.3
in bad/good	health		31.14
be	healthy	for	29.6
be	healthy	from	30.9
to	heap something	on	42.32
to	heap something	with	59.9
to	hear	about	1.1
to	hear	from	30.1
to	hear	of	40.8
out of one's	hearing		46.10
within	hearing		60.4
sick at	heart		11.6
in one's	heart		31.32
in the	heat		31.7
to	heave	against	5.2
to	heave something	up	58.1
down at the	heels		11.11
the	height	of	40.4
under	height		55.3
one's	height is	against	5.5
in a	helicopter		31.1
	help	for	29.1
a	help	to	52.5
beyond	help		20.2
through	help		50.9
to	help	in	31.34
to	help	toward	53.4
to	help someone	(all) through	50.7
to	help	with	59.11
be	helpful	for someone	29.6
be	helpful	to someone	52.5
be	helpful	with	59.5
from	here		30.7
the	hero	of	40.1
the	heroine	of	40.1
to	hide	from	30.10
to	hide something	from	30.2
to	hide	under	55.2
to	hide something	under	55.2
in the game of	hide-and-seek		31.29
in	high heels		31.16
a	highway	to	52.2
down a	highway		25.2
off the	highway		41.3
on the	highway		42.3
on the	highway		42.7
up the	highway		58.4
to	hike	to	52.1
to	hike	toward	53.1

on the	hill		42.2
to	hint	at	11.7
for	hire		29.10
the	hiss	of	40.6
to	hit	against	5.2
to	hit	at	11.3
to	hit	in	31.23
to	hit it	off	41.5
to	hit something	over	48.4
to	hit something	with	59.8
in the game of	hockey		31.29
on	hold		42.28
to	hold	above	2.1
to	hold	against	5.1
to	hold something	on	42.5
to	hold something	over	48.1
to	hold something	over one's head	48.1
to	hold	to	52.8
to	hold	to	52.20
to	hold	up	58.10
to	hold something	up	58.10
through a	hole		50.2
for the	holidays		29.8
over the	holidays		48.9
at	home		11.2
be	honest	with	59.5
on a	honeymoon		42.20
to the	honk	of	52.16
in	honor	of	31.20
of	honor		40.16
on the	honor roll		42.24
to	honor someone	for	29.4
to	hoot	at	11.7
to	hop	off	41.1
to	hop	on	42.8
to	hop	onto	43.1
to	hop	out of	46.3
to	hop	over	48.4
to	hope	for	29.3
in	hordes		31.26
on the	horizon		42.2
to one's	horror		52.5
be	hospitable	to	52.7
be	hospitable	toward	53.2
at a	hospital		11.1
be	hostile	to	52.7
in	hot weather		31.7
at a	hotel		11.1
hour after	hour		4.7

by the	hour		22.4
within the	hour		60.2
over the next few	hours		48.9
at a	house		11.1
on the	house		42.30
all over the	house		48.8
all through the	house		50.6
house to	house		52.11
to	hover	over	48.1
to	howl	at	11.3
the	howl	of	40.6
with a	hug		59.5
to	hum	along with	7.2
the	hum	of	40.6
to the	hum	of	52.16
in the	humidity		31.7
with	humility		59.5
by the	hundreds		22.8
in	hundreds		31.19
in	hundreds		31.26
be	hungry	for	29.3
to	hurry	up	58.10
in a	hurry		31.14
be	hurt	in	31.23
be	hurtful	to	52.5
the	hush	of	40.6
go into	hysterics		36.4
to	ice something	with	59.9
an	idea	for	29.1
an	idea	for	29.3
against an	idea		5.3
behind an	idea		14.5
be far from	ideal		28.2
the	ideas	of	40.1
be	ignorant	of	40.8
be	ignorant	of	40.15
to	ignore someone	(all) through	50.7
of that	ilk	of	40.1
(all) through one's	illness		50.7
be	impatient	for	29.3
be	impatient	with	59.5
be	important	for	29.6
be	important	to	52.5
be	important	to	52.14
be	impossible	for someone	29.6
be	impressed	with	59.6
under the	impression		55.5
the	improvement	in	31.34
in	inches		31.21
on one's	income		42.16
be	inconsiderate	of	40.13
be	inconsiderate	to	52.7
an	increase	in	31.34
with the	increase	in	59.18
be	indebted	to	52.6
with	indifference		59.5
be	indignant	at	11.7
one's	inexperience is	against	5.5
be	inferior	to	52.12
under the	influence	of	55.5
with all one's	influence		59.18
to	inform someone	of	40.8
	information	for	29.1
an	inhabitant	of	40.1
be	inhospitable	toward	53.2
in	ink		31.11
to	insert something	in	31.1
on the	inside	of	42.6
to	install something	over	48.1
on	instinct		42.19
the	instructions	for	29.3
the	instructions	to	52.13
in (the field of)	insurance		31.17
of	integrity		40.16
with all one's	intelligence		59.18
of good/bad	intentions		40.16
be	interested	in	31.34
something/nothing	interesting	about	1.5
on the	interior	of	42.6
on the	Internet		42.17
on the	Internet		42.29
through an	intersection		50.2
to	introduce	to	52.3
to	invest	in	31.34
under	investigation		55.5
an	invoice	for	29.14
be	involved	in	31.17
be	involved	with	59.7
of	iron		40.7
at the	ironing board		11.5
be	irresponsible	of someone	40.15
off the	island		41.3
at	it		11.5
out of	it		46.12
in	italics		31.11
the	jacket	to	52.15
in	jail		31.1
in	jail		31.24
to	jail		52.1
in	jeans		31.16

a	job	for	29.1
by the	job		22.4
to	jog	along	7.1
a	joke	about	1.1
to	joke	about	1.1
in	journalism		31.17
on a	journey		42.20
of	joy		40.6
the	joy	of	40.12
with	joy		59.5
with	joy		59.18
to	judge	between	19.3
to	jump	about	1.6
to	jump	around	9.8
to	jump	back to	12.1
to	jump	in	31.5
to	jump	off	41.1
to	jump	on	42.8
to	jump	onto	43.1
to	jump	out of	46.3
to	jump	over	48.4
to	jump	up	58.1
within a	jurisdiction		60.1
on the	jury		42.24
of	jute		40.7
to	keep	above	2.1
to	keep	against	5.1
to	keep	at it	11.5
to	keep	from	30.9
to	keep someone	from	30.10
to	keep something	from	30.3
to	keep	in	31.36
to	keep	off	41.5
to	keep	on	42.26
to	keep something	on	42.11
to	keep	on ____ing	42.26
to	keep	out (of)	46.13
to	keep	up (with)	58.10
to	keep something	up	58.10
to	keep something	with	59.2
to	keep alive	on	42.16
to	keep away	from	30.3
to	key	in	31.36
the	key	to	52.13
the	key	to	52.15
to	kick someone	around	9.11
to	kick	in	31.23
to	kick	in	31.36
to	kick	off	41.8
to	kick somebody	out	46.1

for	kicks		29.5
to	kill something	off	41.8
in	kilos		31.21
be	kind	about	1.1
a	kind	of	40.4
be	kind	of someone	40.15
be	kind	to	52.7
after one's	kindness		4.4
out of	kindness		46.11
through	kindness		50.9
with	kindness		59.5
under a	king		55.4
with a	kiss		59.5
in a	kitchen		31.1
a	knack	for	29.19
to	kneel	beside	17.1
the	knob	to	52.15
to	knock	against	5.2
to	knock	in	31.23
to	knock something	off	41.8
to	knock	on	42.8
to	knock someone	out	46.13
to	know	about	1.1
to	know something	about	1.1
to	know something	from	30.4
for all one's	knowledge		29.17
be	known	for	29.4
a	lack	of	40.10
be	lacking	in	31.33
on	land		42.3
in (the field of)	landscaping		31.17
by and	large		22.10
at	last		11.4
for	later		29.16
at the	latest		11.10
to	laugh	(all) through	50.7
to	laugh	about	1.1
to	laugh	at	11.3
to	laugh	at	11.7
the	laughter	of	40.6
against the	law		5.3
above the	law		2.6
in (the field of)	law		31.17
within the	law		60.4
on the	lawn		42.2
to	lay something	against	5.1
to	lay something	in	31.1
to	lay something	in	31.5
to	lay	off	41.5
to	lay someone	off	41.8

to	lay something	on	42.12
to	lead someone	toward	53.1
a	leader	of	40.1
to	lean	against	5.1
to	lean	on	42.12
to	lean	over	48.1
to	lean	toward	53.3
to	learn	of	40.8
at	least		11.10
of	leather		40.7
on	leave		42.28
to	leave	for	29.11
to	leave	from	30.1
to	leave something	out	46.1
to	leave	with	59.1
to	leave something	with	59.1
to	leave something	with	59.2
a	lecture	about	1.1
at a	lecture		11.2
in a	lecture		31.1
to	leer	at	11.3
on the	left	of	42.6
in the	leg		31.23
to	lend	to	52.3
a	length	of	40.4
at	length		11.4
through	lenses		50.8
a	lesson	for	29.3
to	let someone	down	25.5
a	letter	for	29.1
a	letter	to	52.2
through the	letters		50.6
be	level	with	59.17
the	lid	to	52.15
to	lie	about	1.1
to	lie	against	5.1
to	lie	around	9.9
to	lie (down)	beside	17.1
to	lie	on	42.12
to	lie	over	48.7
to	lie	under	55.2
in	lieu	of	31.20
for	life		29.15
in	life		31.3
(all) through one's	life		50.7
in	light	of	31.32
through a	light		50.2
a	limit	to	52.20
under the	limit		55.3
within the	limit(s)		60.4
off	limits		41.7
to	limp	across	3.1
to	limp	off	41.1
to	line	up	58.10
in a	line		31.18
in	line		31.18
on	line		42.28
on the	line		42.28
out of	line		46.10
in	lines		31.18
on the	list		42.24
to	listen	to	52.6
from	listening		30.8
	little	of	40.5
a	little	of	40.5
little by	little		22.10
very	little	about	1.1
to	live	across from	3.3
to	live	off	41.6
to	live	on	42.16
to	live	on	42.26
to	live	over	48.7
to	live	through	50.5
to	live	with	59.1
a	load	of	40.4
to	load something	on	42.8
	load something	on	42.32
a	loaf	of	40.4
against one's	loan		5.8
on	loan		42.28
be	located	over	48.7
to	lock up	against	5.7
to	log	on	42.37
to	long	for	29.3
to	look	about	1.6
to	look	after	4.9
to	look	all over the ...	48.8
to	look	around	9.8
to	look	at	11.3
to	look	back to	12.1
to	look	down on	25.5
to	look	for	29.3
to	look	in (on)	31.36
to	look	into	36.1
to	look	into	36.6
to	look	like	37.1
to	look	out (for)	46.13
to	look	over	48.1
to	look	over	48.4
to	look	through	50.6

to	look	toward	53.1	to	make something	out of	46.8
to	look	up to	58.10	to	make	up	58.8
with a	look		59.5	to	make	up (with)	58.10
to	look forward	to	52.22	to	make something	up	58.10
to	look good	with	59.16	to	make something	up to	58.10
to	look something	over	48.14	to	make a pass	at	11.3
to	look something	up	58.10	to	make a toast	to	52.4
to	look up something	under	55.6	to	make do	on	42.16
to	lose weight	on	42.16	in	make-up		31.16
the	loser	of	40.1	out of	malice		46.11
a	lot	of	40.5	at a	mall		11.1
	lots	of	40.5	to	manage	for someone	29.9
be	lousy	at	11.8	under the	management	of	55.4
a	love	of	40.12	the	manager	of	40.1
be in	love	with	59.6	in a	manner		31.15
in	love		31.14	after one's	manners		4.4
out of	love		46.11		many	of	40.5
with	love		59.5	to	march	around	9.8
be	loved	by	22.1	to	march	on	42.27
be	loved	for	29.4	to	march	toward	53.1
in	lower case		31.11	in the	marines		31.17
be	loyal	to	52.7	on the	mark		42.28
out of	loyalty		46.11	on your	mark		42.36
out of	luck		46.6	to	mark something	down	25.5
through	luck		50.9	to	mark something	off	41.8
to	luck	out	46.13	to	mark something	up	58.10
at	lunch		11.2	be	married	to	52.14
for	lunch		29.8	have a	match	with	59.10
over	lunch		48.9	under the	maximum		55.3
(all) through	lunch		50.7	from	May	to September	30.5
to	lunch		52.1	the	mayor	of	40.1
at a	luncheon		11.2	under a	mayor		55.4
towards	lunchtime		54.1	as for	me		10.2
to	lurk	around	9.9	(all) through the	meal		50.7
be above	lying		2.5	be	mean	about	1.1
be beneath	lying		16.3	be	mean	of someone	40.15
on the	machine		42.17	be	mean	to	52.7
be	mad	about	1.2	be	meaningful	to	52.5
like	mad		37.3	above	meanness		2.5
be	made	by	22.1	out of	meanness		46.11
be	made	from	30.7	by all	means		22.10
be	made	of	40.7	the	measurement	of	40.4
be	made up	of	40.7	in	medicine		31.17
in a	magazine		31.1	off one's	medicine		41.4
to	mail	from	30.1	of	meditation		40.9
to	mail something	out	46.2	at a	meeting		11.2
to	make	for	29.1	a	member	of	40.1
to	make something	for	29.13	a	memo	to	52.2
to	make	of	40.4	a	memorial	to	52.4
to	make	out	46.13	in	memory	of	31.20

from	memory		30.8
be	menacing	toward	53.2
to	mention	to	52.3
at one's	mercy		11.11
in a	mess		31.14
a	message	for	29.1
of	metal		40.7
in	meters		31.21
a	method	of	40.1
a	method	of	40.8
on	microfilm		42.15
through a	microscope		50.8
towards	mid-afternoon		54.1
in the	middle	of	40.3
towards	midnight		54.1
by a	mile		22.9
within	miles	of	60.3
in	miles		31.21
in the	military		31.17
in a	million		31.10
make up one's	mind		58.8
be	mindful	of	40.13
under the	minimum		55.3
within	minutes		60.2
with	mirth		59.18
through	misinformation		50.9
to	miss	out on	42.37
on a	mission		42.20
through a	mistake		50.9
to	mix something	up (with)	58.10
to	moan	about	1.1
a	moan	of	40.6
a	moment	of	40.9
at the	moment		11.4
on	Monday (or any day)		42.25
for	money		29.5
out of	money		46.6
with all one's	money		59.18
in	monopoly		31.29
by the	month		22.4
the	month	of	40.9
month after	month		4.7
of the	month		40.1
(all) through the	month		50.7
over the next few	months		48.9
a	monument	to	52.4
in a bad/good	mood		31.14
to	mope	around	9.9
of high/low	morals		40.16

in the	morning		31.3
(all) through the	morning		50.7
on nice	mornings		42.14
	most	of	40.5
at	most		11.10
on a	motorcycle		42.10
in	mourning		31.14
of	mourning		40.9
to	move	about	1.6
to	move	across	3.1
to	move	against	5.3
to	move	against	5.4
to	move	around	9.8
to	move away	from	30.3
to	move	back from	12.2
to	move	back to	12.1
to	move	down	25.1
to	move	down	25.2
to	move	in	31.5
to	move	into	36.1
to	move something	into	36.1
to	move	off	41.1
to	move something	off	41.1
to	move	on	42.26
to	move	onto	43.1
to	move something	onto	43.1
to	move something	out	46.1
to	move something	out of	46.3
to	move	to	52.1
to	move	to tears	52.17
to	move	toward	53.1
to	move	up	58.1
to	move something	up	58.1
to	move something	with	59.8
with the	move	to	59.18
a	movie	about	1.1
at the	movies		11.2
	much	of	40.5
be above	murder		2.5
be beneath	murder		16.3
	music	of	40.1
the	music	of	40.6
to the	music	of	52.16
in	music		31.12
to	nail	to	52.8
to	nail something	over	48.1
to	nail something	with	59.8
to	name someone	after	4.9
the	name	of	40.2
be	nasty	about	1.1

one's	nationality is	against	5.5		through the	notes		50.6
a	native	of	40.1			nothing	for	29.1
by	nature		22.10		for	nothing		29.13
for	naught		29.23		be	notorious	for	29.4
in the	navy		31.17		the	novels	of	40.1
be	necessary	for	29.6		by	now		22.5
a	necessity	of	40.10		in the	nude		31.16
a	need	for	29.3		a	nuisance	to	52.5
a	need	of	40.10		under a	number		55.3
a	need	of	40.12		of	nylon		40.7
in	need		31.14		be	obedient	to	52.7
to	need someone	for	29.3		to	object	to	52.6
through	negligence		50.9		an	objection	to	52.6
to	negotiate	with	59.11		be	objective	about	1.2
all through the	neighborhood		50.6		be	obligated	to	52.14
	neither	of	40.5		be	obnoxious	to	52.5
be	nervous	about	1.2		an	obstacle	to	52.13
in a	nest		31.1		to	obtain	from	30.1
in	neutral		31.24		on the	occasion	of	42.25
the	news	about	1.1		on	occasion		42.14
	news	for	29.1		against all	odds		5.9
on the	news		42.25			off	with	59.20
in a	newspaper		31.1		an	offer	to	52.2
through a	newspaper		50.8		run for	office	for	29.3
be	next	to	52.19		at an	office		11.1
something/nothing	nice	about	1.5		in an	office		31.1
be	nice	about	1.1		in an	office		31.2
be	nice	of someone	40.15		to the	office		52.1
be	nice	to	52.7		in	oil		31.11
in	nickels		31.19		be an	old hand	at	11.8
night after	night		4.7		at	once		11.4
at	night		11.4		for	once		29.23
(all) through the	night		50.7			once and	for all	29.23
on rainy	nights		42.14		one by	one		22.10
in the	nineties		31.3		after	one's own heart		4.8
in	no time		31.4		beyond	one's wildest dreams		20.2
to	nod	off	41.8		in	ones		31.19
to	nod one's head	in	31.25		beside	oneself		17.2
the	noise	of	40.6		(all) by	oneself		22.10
to the	noise	of	52.16		be	open	to	52.7
to	nominate	as	10.1		be	open	with	59.5
to	nominate someone	for	29.3		to	open something	with	59.8
against a	nomination		5.3		to	operate	for someone	29.9
	none	of	40.5		the	opinion	of	40.1
towards	noon		54.1		in one's	opinion		31.32
under the	norm		55.3		with	optimism		59.5
above	normal		2.2		be	optimistic	about	1.2
a	nose	for	29.19		(all) through the	ordeal		50.7
by a	nose		22.9		in	order		31.18
in a	notebook		31.1					

in	order	to	31.20
on	order		42.28
out of	order		46.10
on the	orders	of	42.19
against	orders		5.3
under	orders		55.4
out of the	ordinary		46.7
of an	organization	of	40.1
by the	ounce		22.5
in	ounces		31.21
after one's	outburst		4.4
on an	outing		42.20
on the	outside	of	42.6
on the	outskirts	of	42.6
to	pass someone	over	48.14
on one's	own		42.28
to	pack something	with	59.9
a	package	of	40.4
by the	package		22.5
on the	page	of	42.6
on	page one, two, etc.		42.3
a	pain	in one's	31.23
a	pain	in the neck	31.23
in	pain		31.14
in	pain		31.25
to	paint	with	59.8
to	paint something	over	48.5
to	paint something	with	59.8
to	paint something	with	59.9
the	paintings	of	40.1
beyond the	pale		20.4
a	paper	on	42.21
of	paper		40.7
on	paper		42.15
through the	papers		50.6
be on a	par	with	59.17
at a	parade		11.2
be	parallel	to	52.19
be	parallel	with	59.17
at a	park		11.1
in	park		31.24
through the	park		50.1
to the	park		52.1
at a	parking lot		11.1
on	parole		42.28
the	part	to	52.15
to	part	with	59.15
to	part company	with	59.15
to	participate	in	31.34
in	particular		31.32

a	partnership	with	59.11
in	partnership	with	59.11
in	parts		31.8
into	parts		36.3
at a	party		11.2
to	pass something	in	31.5
to	pass something	on	42.37
to	pass	on something	1.1
to	pass	out	46.13
to	pass something	out	46.2
to	pass out	among	8.3
to	pass someone	over	48.14
to	pass	to	52.3
to	pass something	up	58.10
through a	passage		50.1
out of	passion		46.11
in the	past		31.3
out of the	past		46.12
to	paste	to	52.8
to	paste something	on	42.5
a	path	to	52.2
down a	path		25.2
on the	path		42.3
up the	path		58.4
be	patient	with	59.5
on the	patio		42.2
a	pattern	for	29.3
a	pattern	of	40.4
the	paucity	of	40.10
to	pay something/someone	back	12.3
to	pay someone	for	29.4
behind in	payments		14.4
on the	payroll		42.24
at	peace		11.6
for	peace		29.5
something/nothing	peculiar	about	1.5
in	pencil		31.11
in	pennies		31.19
the	people	of	40.1
about	perfect		1.7
be far from	perfect		28.2
to	perform	for	29.1
(all) through the	performance		50.7
a	period	of	40.9
through a	periscope		50.8
be above	perjury		2.5
be beneath	perjury		16.3
be	perpendicular	to	52.19
to	persist	in	31.34

in	person		31.15
to	pertain	to	52.14
be	pertinent	to	52.14
be	pessimistic	about	1.2
to	petition	for	29.3
a	petition	to	52.2
to	pick	as	10.1
to	pick	at	11.12
to	pick	between	19.3
to	pick	off	41.2
to	pick	on	42.34
to	pick	on	42.37
to	pick something	out	46.13
to	pick something	over	48.14
to	pick	up	58.10
to	pick something	up	58.10
a	picture	of	40.6
a	piece	of	40.4
by the	piece		22.4
in	pieces		31.8
into	pieces		36.3
in a	pile		31.18
	pile something	on	42.32
in	piles		31.18
to	pin	to	52.8
by the	pint		22.5
through a	pipe		50.1
have	pity	on	42.33
out of	pity		46.11
to	place	above	2.1
to	place	against	5.1
from one	place	to another	30.5
in	place		31.1
out of	place		46.7
all over the	place		48.8
place to	place		52.11
to	place something	in	31.1
to	place something	in	31.5
to	place something	into	36.1
to	place something	over	48.1
to	place something	over	48.5
to	place something	under	55.2
a	plan	for	29.1
a	plan	for	29.3
to	plan	for	29.11
against a	plan		5.3
behind a	plan		14.5
to	plant something	with	59.9
a	plaque	to	52.4
of	plastic		40.7

a	plate	of	40.4
of	platinum		40.7
to	play	(all) through	50.7
to	play	about	1.1
to	play	against	5.3
to	play	along with	7.2
to	play	among	8.2
to	play	around	9.8
to	play	for	29.1
to	play	like	37.2
to	play	with	59.1
at a	play		11.2
(all) through the	play		50.7
to	play a game	with	59.1
all over the	playground		48.8
the	plays	of	40.1
to	plead	for	29.3
be	pleasant	to	52.7
be	pleased	for someone	29.7
be	pleased	with	59.6
be	pleasing	to	52.5
the	pleasure	of	40.12
for	pleasure		29.5
with	pleasure		59.5
	plenty	of	40.5
behind a	plot		14.5
to	plow something	with	59.8
the	poems	of	40.1
the	poetry	of	40.1
in	poetry		31.12
to	point	toward	53.1
beside the	point		17.2
from one's	point of view		30.7
to	point something	out to	46.13
to	poke	about	1.6
to	poke	in	31.23
under a	policy		55.4
be	polite	to	52.7
in	politics		31.17
in the game of	polo		31.29
of	polyester		40.7
in	ponytails		31.16
be	poor	in	31.33
to	pop	up	58.1
be	popular	for	29.4
for all one's	popularity		29.17
on the	porch		42.2
in	portions		31.8
from a	position		30.7
be	possible	for someone	29.6

to	pounce	on	42.8
to	pound	on	42.8
by the	pound		22.5
in	pounds		31.21
to	pour something	in	31.5
to	pour something	into	36.1
to	pour something	on	42.8
to	pour something	out of	46.3
to	pour something	over	48.5
have	power	over	48.6
in	power		31.24
with all one's	power		59.18
at a	practice		11.2
for	practice		29.5
for	practice		29.10
in	practice		31.30
out of	practice		46.7
a	practitioner	of	40.1
in	praise	of	31.20
to	praise someone	for	29.4
to	pray	about	1.1
to	pray	for	29.3
of	prayer		40.9
in one's	prayers		31.3
against the	precepts		5.3
be	precious	to	52.5
be	predicated	on	42.13
to	prefer	to	52.6
be	preferable	to	52.5
be	preferable	to	52.12
a	preference	for	29.21
on the	premise	of	42.19
be	prepared	for	29.3
in one's	presence		31.15
a	present	for	29.1
a	present	to	52.2
to	present	to	52.3
a	present	to	52.4
at	present		11.4
to	preside	over	48.6
under the	presidency	of	55.4
the	president	of	40.1
under a	president		55.4
to	press	on	42.26
to	press	to	52.8
put	pressure	on	42.34
to	prevent someone	from	30.10
to	prey	on	42.34
the	price	of	40.4
at a	price		11.9

with	pride		59.5
under a	principal		55.4
against the	principles		5.3
in	print		31.11
in	private		31.15
with the	problems		59.18
with all one's	problems		59.19
by	profession		22.10
a	professor	of	40.1
under a	professor		55.4
a	program	about	1.1
a	program	for	29.3
at a	program		11.2
a	project	for	29.1
a	project	for	29.3
behind a	project		14.5
with a	promise		59.5
be	promised	to	52.14
a	proposal	to	52.2
against a	proposal		5.3
at the	prospect	of	11.4
to	protect	against	5.7
to	protect something	from	30.3
be	proud	of	40.8
be	proud	of	40.13
be	provided	with	59.4
in	public		31.15
in	publishing		31.17
to	pull	against	5.1
to	pull	back to	12.1
to	pull	down	25.2
to	pull something	in	31.5
to	pull	into	36.2
to	pull	off	41.2
to	pull something	off	41.1
to	pull something	off	41.8
to	pull something	out of	46.3
to	pull	over	48.14
to	pull something	over	48.5
to	pull something	over	48.14
to	pull something	through	50.2
to	pull something	toward	53.1
to	pull a gun/knife	on	42.27
to	punch	in	31.23
to	punish someone	for	29.4
for	purchase		29.10
on	purpose		42.19
to	push	against	5.2
to	push	back to	12.1
to	push	down	25.2

to	push	for	29.21
to	push something	in	31.1
to	push something	in	31.5
to	push	into	36.2
to	push something	off	41.1
to	push something	on	42.32
to	push something	out of	46.3
to	push something	through	50.2
to	push	toward	53.3
to	push something	toward	53.1
to	push	to the limits	52.17
to	push something	under	55.2
be	put	out	46.12
to	put	above	2.1
to	put	against	5.1
to	put	around	9.3
to	put something	back	12.3
to	put something	by	22.11
to	put something	down	25.5
to	put something	in	31.1
to	put something	in	31.5
to	put something	into	36.1
to	put something	off	41.8
to	put something	on	42.8
to	put something	on	42.11
	put something	on	42.32
to	put something	out	46.3
to	put something	over	48.5
to	put something	under	55.2
to	put	up with	59.21
to	put something	with	59.2
to	put together	from	30.6
to	puzzle	over	48.10
for all one's	qualifications		29.17
to	quarrel	with	59.10
have a	quarrel	with	59.10
by the	quart		22.5
in	quarters		31.19
to	question	about	1.1
a	question	for	29.1
a	question	to	52.2
in	question		31.32
with a	question		59.5
of	quiet		40.9
to	race	around	9.1
to	race	back to	12.1
of a	race	of	40.1
a	race	to	52.2
to	race	up	58.1
in the game of	racquetball		31.29

on the	radio		42.29
in a	rage		31.14
with	rage		59.18
a	raid	on	42.27
to	rain	on	42.8
in the	rain		31.7
with the	rain		59.18
in	rainy weather		31.7
to	ram something	in	31.5
within	range		60.4
to	rat	on	42.35
of	rayon		40.7
out of	reach		46.7
within	reach		60.4
to	react	in	31.25
to	react	to	52.6
a	reaction	to	52.6
after one's	reaction		4.4
in	reaction		31.25
to	read	about	1.1
to	read	on	42.26
to	read	to	52.3
to	read something	over	48.11
at a	reading		11.2
of	reading		40.9
be	ready	for	29.3
about	ready		1.7
by the	ream		22.5
to	rebel	at	11.7
a	receipt	for	29.14
on	receipt		42.31
to	receive	from	30.1
to	receive something	through	50.2
a	recipe	for	29.3
to	recommend	to	52.3
on the	recommendation	of	42.19
on	reconnaissance		42.19
off the	record		41.7
on	record		42.15
on	record		42.28
through the	records		50.6
through	red tape		50.5
of	reflection		40.9
on	reflection		42.31
with	regard		59.5
to	register	for	29.3
against the	regulations		5.3
to	reimburse someone	for	29.4
to	rejoice	at	11.7
to	relate	to	52.6

be	related	to	52.14		to	rest	on	42.12
a	relation	to	52.6		to	rest	under	55.2
a	relationship	with	59.11		at a	restaurant		11.1
for	relaxation		29.5		to	restrict	to	52.20
to	release something	from	30.2		a	restriction	on	42.22
be	relevant	to	52.14		in	return		31.30
in	relief		31.25		in	return		31.32
of	relief		40.6		to	return	to	52.1
to	relieve someone	of	40.11		at a	reunion		11.2
of a	religion	of	40.1		to	reveal	to	52.3
against a	religion		5.3		in	reverse		31.24
to	rely	on	42.13		in	reverse		31.32
a	remark	to	52.4		to	revert	to	52.6
to	remind someone	about	1.1		to	reward someone	for	29.4
to	remind someone	of	40.8		a	rhythm	for	29.19
be	reminiscent	of	40.8		to the	rhythm	of	52.16
to	remove something	from	30.3		in	rhythm	with	31.22
for	rent		29.10		in	rhythm		31.12
to	rent something	for	29.13		be	rich	in	31.33
be	repentant	of	40.8		be	rich	in	31.34
be	repentant	of	40.13		be/get	rid	of	40.11
to	reply	to	52.6		to	ride	across	3.1
a	reply	to	52.6		to	ride	around	9.1
to	report	about	1.1		to	ride	down	25.2
a	report	on	42.21		to	ride	on	42.9
to	report	on	42.21		to	ride	to	52.1
to	reprimand someone	for	29.4		to	ride	with	59.14
be	repulsive	to	52.5		be	ridiculous	for someone	29.6
by	reputation		22.10		be	right	about	1.2
a	request	for	29.14		on the	right	of	42.6
a	request	to	52.2		about	right		1.7
on	request		42.19		on the	rink		42.3
to one's	rescue		52.4		to	rip something	out of	46.3
the	research	on	42.21		to	rise	to the occasion	52.1
in	research		31.17		at	risk		11.6
in the	reserves		31.17		on the	river		42.7
to	reside	over	48.7		a	road	to	52.2
a	resident	of	40.1		down a	road		25.2
show	respect	for	29.21		off the	road		41.3
out of	respect		46.11		on the	road		42.3
be	respectful	of	40.13		on the	road		42.7
be	respectful	to	52.7		on the	road		42.28
to	respond	to	52.6		up the	road		58.3
a	response	to	52.6		up the	road		58.4
be	responsible	of someone	40.15		to the	roar	of	52.16
at	rest		11.6		be above	robbing		2.5
of	rest		40.9		to	rock	to sleep	52.17
to	rest	against	5.1		off one's	rocker		41.4
to	rest	beside	17.1		on the	rocks		42.3

to	roll	all over the …	48.8
to	roll	down	25.1
to	roll	off	41.1
to	roll something	off	41.1
on a	roll		42.28
on	roller blades		42.10
on the	roof		42.2
	room	for	29.2
in a	room		31.1
up and down the	room		58.8
be	rough	on	42.34
to	round	up	58.6
to	round something	off	41.8
to	row	up	58.5
in a	row		31.18
in	rows		31.18
be	rude	about	1.1
be	rude	of someone	40.15
in for a	rude awakening		31.31
in	ruins		31.14
to	rule	over	48.6
against the	rules		5.3
by the	rules		22.4
within the	rules		60.4
to	run	about	1.6
to	run	across	3.1
to	run	across	3.5
to	run	after	4.3
to	run	against	5.4
to	run	all over the …	48.8
to	run	along	7.1
to	run	along with	7.2
to	run	around	9.1
to	run	around	9.8
to	run	around with	9.11
to	run away	from	30.3
to	run	back from	12.2
to	run	back to	12.1
to	run something	by	22.11
to	run	down	25.1
to	run	down	25.2
to	run something	down	25.5
to	run	for	29.3
to	run	for someone	29.9
to	run	in	31.5
to	run	into	36.1
to	run	into	36.2
to	run	into	36.6
to	run something	into the ground	36.2

to	run	off	41.1
to	run something	off	41.1
to	run	on	42.16
to	run	on	42.26
to	run	onto	43.1
to	run	out of	46.3
to	run	out of	46.6
to	run	over	48.4
to	run	to	52.1
to	run	toward	53.1
to	run	up	58.1
to	run something	up	58.10
to go for a	run		29.23
the	run-around		9.10
to	rush	at	11.3
the	rush	of	40.6
on	sabbatical		42.19
in a	sack		31.1
in	sadness		31.25
of	sadness		40.6
with	sadness		59.5
on a	safari		42.20
to	sail	against	5.4
to	sail	from	30.1
to	sail	into	36.1
to	sail	toward	53.1
to	sail	up	58.5
to	sail	with	59.14
on one's	salary		42.16
a	sale	on	42.22
for	sale		29.10
on	sale		42.28
beyond	salvation		20.2
of	sand		40.7
be	sassy	to	52.7
to one's	satisfaction		52.5
be	satisfied	with	59.6
be	satisfying	to	52.5
on	Saturdays (et al.)		42.14
to	save something	from	30.3
beyond	saving		20.2
to	saw	off	41.2
to	say	about	1.1
to go without	saying		61.5
a	scarcity	of	40.10
to	scare something	from	30.3
be	scattered	about	1.4
behind the	scenes		14.6
behind	schedule		14.4
on	schedule		42.28

behind a	scheme		14.5
a	scholarship	to	52.4
at	school		11.2
in	school		31.1
off	school		41.4
through (with)	school		50.5
to	school		52.1
to	scold someone	for	29.4
on a	scooter		42.10
to	scrape by	on	42.16
to	scrape something	off	41.1
a	scratch	in	31.23
to	scream	about	1.1
to	scream	for	29.3
to	scream	in	31.25
be	screaming	with	59.18
on the	screen		42.3
to	screw	to	52.8
to	sculpt something	out of	46.8
to	seal	against	5.7
to	search	around	9.8
in	search	of	31.20
the	season	of	40.9
in	season		31.13
out of	season		46.7
to	season something	with	59.8
on	second thought		42.31
be	seconded	to	52.14
a	secret	for	29.1
the	secret	to	52.13
a	secretary	of	40.1
the	secretary	to	52.15
in	sections		31.8
for	security		29.5
to	see	about	1.1
to	see	for oneself	29.23
to	see	through	50.3
to	see	to	52.22
to	see someone	through	50.10
to	seem	like	37.1
to	select	as	10.1
to	select	between	19.3
be	selfish	of someone	40.15
through	selfishness		50.9
to	sell something	for	29.13
to	sell something	off	41.8
the	semester	of	40.9
to	send something	all over the …	48.8
to	send	back	12.3
to	send	for	29.3

to	send someone	for	29.3
to	send	from	30.1
to	send	off	41.2
to	send something	out	46.2
to	send something	through	50.2
to	send	to	52.1
to	send	to	52.3
to	send something	up	58.1
a	sense	of	40.4
a	sense	of	40.6
to	sentence	to	52.20
to	separate something	from	30.3
to	separate	in/into	31.8
to	separate	into	36.3
in	September (et al.)		31.3
in all	seriousness		31.32
a	servant	of	40.1
to	serve	as	10.1
to	serve	with	59.8
to	serve something	with	59.8
in a	session	with	31.22
in	session		31.24
to	set	above	2.1
to	set	against	5.1
to	set something	into	36.1
to	set	up	58.10
to	set something	up	58.10
to	set out	for	29.11
in the	seventies		31.3
to	sever	in/into	31.8
to	sever relations	with	59.15
	several	of	40.5
to	sew	to	52.8
to	sew something	out of	46.8
to	sew something	over	48.5
at the	sewing machine		11.5
be	sewn	from	30.7
to	shake one's head	in	31.25
with	shame		59.5
with	shame		59.18
a	shape	of	40.4
in	shape		31.14
get into	shape		36.4
be out of	shape		46.7
to	shape something	out of	46.8
to	share something	among	8.2
to	shave	off	41.2
to	shield something	from	30.3
to	shine	over	48.1

to	ship	to	52.1
on a	ship		42.9
in for a	shock		31.31
be	shocked	at	11.7
in	shoes		31.16
to	shoot	at	11.3
to	shop	around	9.8
to	shop	for	29.3
in	short		31.12
in	shorts		31.16
to	shout	at	11.3
to	shout	for	29.3
a	shout	of	40.6
to	shout	to	52.3
be	shouting	with	59.18
to	shove something	in	31.5
to	shove something	off	41.1
to	shove something	toward	53.1
to	shovel something	off	41.1
to	show	around	9.11
to	show	to	52.3
to	show	up	58.10
at a	show		11.2
to	show someone	around	9.11
to	show	through	50.3
to	show someone	through	50.10
to	show someone	up	58.10
to	shower something	on	42.8
with a	shudder		59.5
to	shut	off	41.6
to	shut something	off	41.6
to	shut	down	25.5
be	sick	about	1.2
be	sick	from	30.9
be	sick	of	40.8
in	sickness		31.3
in	sickness		31.14
on the	side	of	42.6
from one	side	to the other	30.5
be on one's	side		42.12
side to	side		52.11
down a	sidewalk		25.2
on the	sidewalk		42.3
all over the	sidewalk		48.8
a	sigh	of	40.6
to	sigh	over	48.10
with a	sigh		59.5
the	sight	of	40.6
in	sight		31.35
on	sight		42.31

out of	sight		46.10
within	sight		60.4
a	sign	of	40.8
to	sign	off	41.8
to	sign	up	58.10
to	sign someone	up	58.10
the	silence	of	40.6
of	silence		40.9
in	silence		31.15
of	silk		40.7
be	silly	about	1.2
of	silver		40.7
be	similar	to	52.12
to	sing	about	1.1
to	sing	along with	7.2
to	sing	for	29.1
to	sing	like	37.2
to	sing	of	40.8
to	sing	to	52.3
to	sing	to sleep	52.17
to	sink	to	52.1
to	sip something	out of	46.3
to	sit	(all) through	50.7
to	sit	across from	3.3
to	sit	around	9.9
to	sit	in back of	12.4
to	sit	on	42.12
to	sit	under	55.2
to	sit (down)	beside	17.1
in a	situation	with	31.22
in the	sixties		31.3
a	size	of	40.4
to	skate	down	25.2
to	skate	over	48.4
on a	skateboard		42.10
on	skates		42.10
with	skill		59.5
be	skilled	at	11.8
to	skip	around	9.1
to	skip	over	48.4
in a	skirt		31.16
on	skis		42.10
to	slap	at	11.3
a	slap	in	31.23
on a	sled		42.10
to	sleep	(all) through	50.7
to	sleep	against	5.1
to	sleep	beside	17.1
to	sleep	on	42.12
to	sleep	under	55.2

into	slices		36.3
to	slide	down	25.1
to	slide	off	41.1
to	slide something	off	41.1
to	slip	off	41.1
to	slip something	off	41.1
to	slip	up	58.10
through a	slot		50.2
to	smash	into	36.2
to	smash	to bits	52.17
to	smear something	on	42.8
to	smear something	with	59.9
the	smell	of	40.4
the	smell	of	40.6
to	smile	at	11.3
to	smile	in	31.25
a	smile	of	40.6
with a	smile		59.5
be	smiling	with	59.18
with a	smirk		59.5
through the	smoke		50.3
over	snacks		48.9
to	snatch	at	11.3
to	sneer	in	31.25
to	snoop	around	9.8
be above	snooping		2.5
to	snort	at	11.7
in the	snow		31.7
with	snow		59.18
on a	snowboard		42.10
to	soak	to the skin	52.17
of a	society	of	40.1
in a	society		31.2
be	soft	on	42.34
in the game of	solitaire		31.29
the	solution	to	52.13
	some	of	40.5
	something	for	29.1
the	songs	of	40.1
be	sore	from	30.9
in a	sorority		31.2
in	sorrow		31.25
be	sorry	for someone	29.7
a	sort	of	40.4
at the	sound	of	11.4
the	sound	of	40.4
the	sound	of	40.6
to the	sound	of	52.16
to	speak	for someone	29.9
to	speak	of	40.8

to	speak	on	42.21
to	speak	to	52.3
on	spec		42.19
something/nothing	special	about	1.5
of a	species	of	40.1
a	speech	about	1.1
a	speech	on	42.21
in a	speech		31.1
be	speechless	at	11.7
at a	speed		11.9
on high/low	speed		42.28
to	spend a period of time	with	59.1
to	spill	onto	43.1
to	spill something	on	42.8
to	spill something	onto	43.1
to	spill something	all over the …	48.8
to	spin	around	9.2
in	spite	of	31.32
out of	spite		46.11
be	spiteful	toward	53.2
to	splash	against	5.2
to	splash something	on	42.8
to	split	in/into	31.8
to	split	up with	59.15
on the	spot		42.28
to	spray something	on	42.8
to	spread something	on	42.8
to	spread something	over	48.5
to	spread something	with	59.9
on a	spree		42.28
in (the)	spring		31.3
to	sprinkle something	on	42.8
to	sprinkle something	with	59.9
be	sprinkled	about	1.4
on the	squad		42.24
to	squeal	in	31.25
to	squeeze someone	in	31.36
to	squeeze something	in	31.5
to	squeeze something	out of	46.3
to	squirt something	on	42.8
in a	stack		31.18
in	stacks		31.18
on the	staff		42.24
on the	stairs		42.4
to	stamp	on	42.8
to	stand	beside	17.1
to	stand	by	22.11
to	stand	for	29.21
to not	stand	for	29.24

to	stand in	for someone	29.9
to	stand in line	for	29.3
to	stand	on	42.12
to	stand	out (from)	46.13
to	stand	under	55.2
to	stand	up	58.10
to	stand someone	up	58.9
to	stand up	for	29.21
to	stand up	for	29.24
on	stand-by		42.28
to	staple	to	52.8
the	star	of	40.1
to	stare	at	11.3
to	stare	into	36.1
from	start	to finish	30.6
to	start	with	59.12
to	start out	for	29.11
to	start	(over) from	30.2
to	start something	over	48.11
to	starve	to death	52.17
be	starved	for	29.3
in a	state		31.1
all over the	state		48.8
through the	state		50.1
all through the	state		50.6
within a	state		60.1
a	statement	about	1.1
a	statement	to	52.4
at a	station		11.1
to	stay	(all) through	50.7
to	stay	off	41.5
to	stay	with	59.1
to	steal something	from	30.3
above	stealing		2.5
be beneath	stealing		16.3
be	steeped	in	31.34
to	step	in	31.36
to	step	on	42.8
to	step	onto	43.1
to	step	out of	46.3
to	step	out of	46.13
to	step	over	48.4
to	step	up	58.10
to	step something	up	58.10
in	step	with	31.22
on the	steps		42.4
in a	stew		31.14
to	stick	to	52.8
to	stick something	on	42.5
to	stick up one's nose	in	31.25

be	stiff	with	59.5
out of	stock		46.6
in	stocks and bonds		31.17
in the	stomach		31.23
to	stomp	into	36.1
through a	stop sign		50.2
to	stop someone	from	30.10
at a	store		11.1
to	store something	under	55.2
to	store something	with	59.2
to	storm	into	36.1
in the	storm		31.7
a	story	about	1.1
at the	stove		11.5
something/nothing	strange	about	1.5
the	strap	to	52.15
through a	straw		50.1
down a	street		25.2
off the	street		41.3
on the	street		42.3
on the	street		42.7
all over the	street		48.8
up the	street		58.3
up the	street		58.4
of	strength		40.16
the	stress	of	40.12
be	strewn	about	1.4
be	strict	on	42.34
to	strike	down	25.3
to	strike	in	31.23
on	strike		42.28
have two	strikes	against	5.9
of	string		40.7
to	strive	for	29.3
to	stroll	along	7.1
to	struggle	against	5.4
to	struggle	through	50.5
to the	strum	of	52.16
a	student	of	40.1
	study	for	29.3
to	study	with	59.1
from	studying		30.9
of	studying		40.9
to	stuff something	with	59.9
to	stumble	on	42.18
to	stumble	over	48.4
a	style	of	40.4
in	style		31.13
out of	style		46.7
be	submerged	in	31.34

glossary

to	submit	to	52.3		be	sympathetic	with	59.5
to	subscribe	to	52.21		to	sympathize	with	59.11
to	substitute	as	10.1		in	sympathy	with	31.22
to	substitute	for someone	29.9		in	sympathy	with	59.11
to	subtract something	from	30.3		out of	sympathy		46.11
					with	sympathy		59.5
a	subway	to	52.2		in	sync		31.12
after one's	success		4.4		out of	sync		46.7
to	suffer	from	30.9		a	system	for	29.3
to	suffer	through	50.5		at a	table		11.1
to	suggest	to	52.3		all over the	table		48.8
a	suggestion	for	29.1		by the	tablespoonful		22.5
a	suggestion	to	52.2		in (the game of)	tag		31.29
against a	suggestion		5.3		to	take	after	4.9
in a	suit		31.16		to	take away	from	30.3
in a	suitcase		31.1		to	take	back	12.3
in (the)	summer		31.3		to	take something back	to/from	12.3
over the	summer		48.9					
in the	sun		31.7		to	take	back to	12.1
in the	sunshine		31.7		to	take	down	25.2
be	superior	to	52.12		to	take	down	25.3
under	supervision		55.4		to	take someone	for	29.24
under a	supervisor		55.4		to	take something	for	29.13
be	sure	of	40.13		to	take something	from	30.3
on the	surface	of	42.6		to	take something	in	31.5
on a	surfboard		42.10		to	take something	in	31.36
a	surprise	for	29.1		to	take	off	41.2
in for a	surprise		31.31		to	take	off	41.8
of	surprise		40.6		to	take	off (from)	30.2
to one's	surprise		52.5		to	take something	off	41.1
be	surprised	at	11.7		to	take something	off	41.8
under	surveillance		55.4		to	take off	for	29.11
to	survive	on	42.16		to	take	on	42.32
to	suspend something	over	48.1		to	take something	out	46.1
					to	take something	out of	46.3
under	suspicion		55.5		to	take	over (from)	48.14
be	suspicious	of	40.13		to	take something	over	48.14
to	swear	at	11.3		to	take something	through	50.2
to	swear	by	22.11		to	take	to	52.3
to	sweep	with	59.8		to	take something	up	58.1
to	sweep something	off	41.1		to	take something	up	58.10
to	sweep something	with	59.8		to	take steps	toward	53.3
be	sweet	about	1.1		a	talent	for	29.19
be	sweet	of someone	40.15		with all one's	talent		59.18
to	swim	across	3.1		to	talk	(all) through	50.7
to	swim	against	5.4		to	talk	about	1.1
to	swim	up	58.5		to	talk	among	8.2
go for a	swim		29.23		to	talk someone	into	36.6
to	swing	at	11.3		to	talk	like	37.2
to	switch something	off	41.6		to	talk	of	40.8

to	talk	on	42.26
to	talk someone	out of	46.13
to	talk	with	59.1
on	tap		42.28
to	tape	to	52.8
on	tape		42.15
to	tape something	over	48.5
on	target		42.28
the	taste	of	40.4
the	taste	of	40.6
to	tattle	on	42.35
a	tax	on	42.22
over	tea		48.9
to	teach	about	1.1
to	teach	for someone	29.9
a	teacher	of	40.1
under a	teacher		55.4
in	teaching		31.17
against the	teachings		5.3
against a	team		5.3
on the	team		42.24
to	tear something	down	25.3
to	tear	into	36.2
to	tear something	off	41.2
to	tear something	out	46.1
to	tear something	out of	46.3
to	tear	to pieces	52.17
to	tear	to shreds	52.17
to	tear	up	58.8
to	tear something	up	58.10
	tears	of	40.6
in	tears		31.14
with	tears		59.18
to	tease someone	for	29.4
by the	teaspoonful		22.5
in a	tee shirt		31.16
off the	telephone		41.4
on the	telephone		42.17
over the	telephone		48.12
on	television		42.29
to	tell	about	1.1
to	tell something	from	30.4
to	tell someone	of	40.8
to	tell	on	42.35
to	tell	to	52.3
one in	ten		31.10
with	tenderness		59.5
in (the game of)	tennis		31.29
in	tens		31.19
in	terms	of	31.32

on the	terrace		42.2
be	terrible	at	11.8
within a	territory		60.1
the	texture	of	40.4
the	texture	of	40.6
with a	thank you		59.5
be	thankful	for	29.6
be	thankful	to	52.6
with	thanks		59.5
of	thanksgiving		40.9
at	that		11.11
at a	theater		11.1
be above	theft		2.5
in	theory		31.32
from	there		30.7
a	thesis	on	42.21
through the	things		50.6
to	think	about	1.1
to	think	back to	12.1
to	think	of	40.8
to	think something	over	48.14
to	think	up	58.7
be	thirsty	for	29.3
at the	thought	of	11.4
be	thoughtful	of	40.15
be	thoughtless	of	40.15
	thoughts	on	42.21
in one's	thoughts		31.3
by the	thousands		22.8
in	thousands		31.26
a	threat	to	52.13
be	thrilled	at	11.7
be	thrilled	for someone	29.7
be	thrilled	with	59.6
to	thrive	on	42.16
be	through	with	59.15
about	through		1.7
to	throw	against	5.2
to	throw something	all over the …	48.8
to	throw	at	11.3
to	throw something	in	31.5
to	throw something	into	36.1
to	throw something	off	41.2
to	throw something	on	42.8
to	throw something	out	46.1
to	throw something	over	48.4
to	throw something	toward	53.1
to	throw	up	58.10
be	thrown	about	1.4
to	thrust	against	5.2

the	ticket	to	52.15
against the	tide		5.4
with the	tide		59.14
in a	tie	with	31.16
to	tie something	around	9.3
to	tie something	to	52.20
be	tied	to	52.14
be	tied	with	59.17
be	tied up	with	59.1
a	time	of	40.9
about	time		1.8
time after	time		4.7
at a	time		11.4
by the	time		22.5
on	time		42.36
out of	time		46.6
(all) through the	time		50.7
from time to	time		52.21
with	time		59.13
for the	time being		29.23
behind the	times		14.6
of	tin		40.7
on	tiptoe		42.10
be	tired	from	30.9
be	tired	of	40.8
a	toast	to	52.4
on the tip of one's	tongue		42.36
be	too hard	for someone	29.6
be	too small	for someone	29.6
at the	top	of	40.3
on the	top	of	42.6
on	top	of	43.2
the	top	to	52.15
from	top	to bottom	30.5
to	toss	at	11.3
a	touch	for	29.19
the	touch	of	40.6
in	touch	with	31.22
out of	touch	with	46.10
be	tough	on	42.34
about	town		1.4
in a	town		31.1
all over the	town		48.8
through (the)	town		50.1
all through the	town		50.6
be out of	town		46.4
be in	town		31.1
around a	track		9.1
on	track		42.28
to	trade something	for	29.13
against	traffic		5.4
with the	traffic		59.14
with the	traffic		59.18
the	train	for	29.3
to	train	on	42.16
a	train	to	52.2
on a	train		42.9
for all one's	training		29.17
in	training		31.17
through	training		50.5
to	transfer something	onto	43.1
through a	translator		50.8
to	travel	all over the …	48.8
to	travel	around	9.1
to	travel	on	42.9
to	travel	with	59.1
to	tread	on	42.8
above	treason		2.5
the	treasurer	of	40.1
in for a	treat		31.31
to	tremble	at	11.7
to	tremble	in	31.25
be	trembling	with	59.18
on	trial		42.28
on a	tricycle		42.10
to	trip	on	42.18
to	trip	over	48.4
a	trip	to	52.2
on a	trip		42.20
in	trouble		31.14
in	trouble		31.24
get into	trouble		36.4
through	trouble		50.5
with the	trouble		59.18
in	trouble	with	31.22
by the	truckload		22.8
in	truckloads		31.26
in a	trunk		31.1
in	trust		31.15
in	trust		31.24
be	trusting	of	40.13
the	truth	about	1.1
in	truth		31.32
be	truthful	with	59.5
to	try something	on	42.11
to	try something	out	46.13
to	try	out (for)	46.13
to	try out	for	29.3
a	tube	of	40.4
to the	tune	of	52.16

in	tune	with	31.12
out of	tune		46.7
through a	tunnel		50.1
to	turn	around	9.2
to	turn something	around	9.2
to	turn something	down	25.5
to	turn	in	31.36
to	turn something	in	31.5
to	turn something	off	41.8
to	turn	on	42.27
to	turn something	on	42.37
to	turn	out	46.13
to	turn	over	48.14
to	turn something	over	48.14
to	turn	toward	53.1
to	turn	up	58.10
to	turn something	up	58.10
down a	turnpike		25.2
off the	turnpike		41.3
up the	turnpike		58.4
in	twenties		31.19
a	type	of	40.4
be	typical	of	40.15
be	unacceptable	to	52.5
be	uncertain	of	40.13
be	uncomfortable	with	59.6
be	unconscionable	of someone	40.15
be	understanding	about	1.1
beyond	understanding		20.2
with	understanding		59.5
be	unfavorable	to	52.5
be	unhappy	about	1.2
be	unhappy	with	59.6
be	unhealthy	for	29.6
in	uniform		31.16
be	unimportant	for someone	29.6
be	unimportant	to	52.5
at a	university		11.1
be	unkind	about	1.1
be	unnecessary	for someone	29.6
be	unsure	of	40.13
something/nothing	unusual	about	1.5
be	unusual	for someone	29.6
be	up	above	2.6
be	up	against	5.1
be	upset	about	1.2
be	upset	at	11.7
be	upset	with	59.6
be	upside	down	25.4
to	use	as	10.1
for	use		29.10
be	used	to	52.6
be	useful	for	29.6
be	useful	for someone	29.6
be	useless	for someone	29.6
be	usual	for someone	29.6
on	vacation		42.19
on	vacation		42.28
to	vaccinate	against	5.7
the	value	of	40.4
from a	vantage point		30.7
in	verse		31.12
be	vexing	to	52.5
in	view	of	31.32
in one's	view		31.32
the	villain	of	40.1
a	vision	of	40.6
in	vogue		31.13
a	voice	for	29.19
in a	voice		31.15
in	volleyball		31.29
on high/low	volume		42.28
to	volunteer	as	10.1
to	vote	against	5.3
toward a	vote		53.3
to	wait	(all) through	50.7
to	wait	for	29.3
to	wait	on	42.34
to	wait	under	55.2
to	wait for someone	(all) through	50.7
to	wait on someone	(all) through	50.7
to	wake	up	58.10
to	wake someone	up	58.10
to	walk	about	1.6
to	walk	across	3.1
to	walk	against	5.4
to	walk	all over the …	48.8
to	walk	along	7.1
to	walk	along with	7.2
to	walk	around	9.1
to	walk	around	9.8
to	walk away	from	30.3
to	walk	back from	12.2
to	walk	back to	12.1
to	walk	beside	17.1
to	walk	down	25.1
to	walk	down	25.2
to	walk	in	31.5
to	walk	into	36.1
to	walk	like	37.2

to	walk	off	41.1
to	walk	on	42.26
to	walk	to	52.1
to	walk	toward	53.1
to	walk	under	55.2
to	walk	up	58.1
to	walk	with	59.1
go for a	walk		29.23
off the	wall		41.7
on the	wall		42.4
within these	walls		60.1
to	wander	about	1.6
to	wander	around	9.8
to	want	for	29.1
to	want someone	for	29.3
to	want something	for	29.13
a	war	on	42.22
at	war		11.6
(all) through the	war		50.7
be	warm	to	52.7
be	warm	toward	53.2
be	wary	of	40.13
to	wash	with	59.8
to	wash something	off	41.1
to	wash something	out (of)	46.13
to	wash something	with	59.8
be	wasteful	for someone	29.6
to	watch	(all) through	50.7
to	watch	out (for)	46.13
to	watch	over	48.1
in hot	water		31.14
like	water		37.3
of	water		40.7
on	water		42.3
in	water colors		31.11
a	way	to	52.2
by the	way		22.10
in a	way		31.15
right of	way		40.17
on the	way		42.28
out of the	way		46.7
up the	way		58.4
to	wear something	off	41.8
to	wear something	on	42.11
to	wear something	out	46.13
to	wear something	over	48.5
to	wear something	under	55.2
at a	wedding		11.2
on one's	wedding		42.25
(all) through the	wedding		50.7

into	wedges		36.3
a	week	of	40.9
by the	week		22.4
week after	week		4.7
(all) through the	week		50.7
on the	weekend		42.25
over the	weekend		48.9
on	weekends		42.14
over the next few	weeks		48.9
to	weep	in	31.25
the	weight	of	40.4
under	weight		55.3
something/nothing	weird	about	1.5
be	well	from	30.9
be	well	off	41.7
be	well-known	for	29.4
at the	wheel		11.5
the	whiff	of	40.6
to	whirl	around	9.2
the	whisper	of	40.6
to	whistle	for	29.3
on the	whole		42.14
the	width	of	40.4
to	win	for	29.1
against the	wind		5.4
with the	wind		59.14
at a	window		11.1
on the	window		42.4
through the	window		50.2
through the	window		50.3
to	wink	at	11.3
the	winner	of	40.1
in (the)	winter		31.3
over the	winter		48.9
to	wipe something	off	41.8
of	wire		40.7
of	wisdom		40.16
to	wish	for	29.3
against one's	wishes		5.3
to	wonder	about	1.1
something/nothing	wonderful	about	1.5
be far from	wonderful		28.2
of	wood		40.7
of	wool		40.7
	word	for word	29.23
with a	word		59.5
	words	of	40.6
	words	of	40.8
of few	words		40.16
to	work	against	5.3

to	work	along with	7.2		be	worse	from	30.9
to	work	as	10.1		be	worse	off	41.7
to	work	beside	17.1		at	worst		11.10
to	work	for	29.1		to	wrap	around	9.3
to	work	for	29.3		to	wrap something	up	58.10
to	work	for someone	29.9		to	wrestle	with	59.10
a	work	of	40.1		to	write	about	1.1
to	work	on	42.26		to	write something	down (on)	25.5
to	work	out	46.13		to	write	for	29.1
to	work	toward	53.3		to	write something	off	41.8
to	work	up	58.6		to	write	on	42.21
to	work	with	59.1		to	write something	over	48.11
to	work	with	59.7		to	write	to	52.3
to	work	with	59.11		to	write something	up	58.10
at	work		11.2		to	write	with	59.8
at	work		11.5		to	write something	with	59.8
of	work		40.9		the	writing	of	40.1
off	work		41.4		all over the	yard		48.8
out of	work		46.6		in	yards		31.21
through with	work		50.5		the	year	of	40.9
through	work		50.9		year after	year		4.7
go to	work		52.1		of the, last/next	year		40.1
to	work something	out	46.13		(all) through the	year		50.7
across the	world		3.4		for	years		29.15
around the	world		9.1		over the next few	years		48.9
all over the	world		48.8		to	yell	about	1.1
be	worried	about	1.2		to	yell	at	11.3
with the	worries		59.18		to	yell	for	29.3
be	worrisome	to	52.5		between	you and me		19.8
to	worry	(all) through	50.7		of one's	youth		40.1
to	worry	about	1.1		one's	youth	is against	5.5
to	worry	over	48.10		with	zeal		59.18
be	worse	for someone	29.6					